RESIDENTIAL SOCIAL WORK
General Editor: Tom Douglas
Staff Support and Staff

Staff Support and Staff Training

Tony Collins and
Terry Bruce

TAVISTOCK PUBLICATIONS
LONDON AND NEW YORK

First published in 1984 by
Tavistock Publications Ltd
11 New Fetter Lane, London
EC4P 4EE

Published in the USA by
Tavistock Publications
in association with Methuen, Inc.
733 Third Avenue, New York,
NY 10017

© 1984 Tony Collins and
Terry Bruce

Printed in Great Britain
by J. W. Arrowsmith Ltd., Bristol

*British Library Cataloguing in
Publication Data*
Bruce, Terry
  Staff support and staff
  training.——
  (Residential social work)
  1. Institutional care
  2. Social service——
  Team work
  I. Title   II. Collins, Terry
  III. Series
  361.4   HV59
  ISBN 0-422-76920-7

*Library of Congress Cataloging
in Publication Data*
Bruce, Terry,
  Staff support and staff training.
  (Residential social work)
  Bibliography: p.
  Includes indexes.
  1. Social group work.
  2. Social work with youth.
  3. Social workers —In-service
    training.
  I.   Collins, Tony.
  II. Title.   III. Series.
  HV45.B78   1984
  361.4   84-2496
  ISBN 0-422-76920-7

Contents

General Editor's Foreword

In a very direct sense residential work is team work. The method of creating an environment in which care, learning, and change can take place is almost wholly dependent for success upon the professional staff working to a clear and accepted pattern. This often requires suspending differences of outlook and approach in order to present a united effort. It follows from this that the concept of loyalty to the chosen approach must be a very high priority for residential staff. That this should not be a blind loyalty goes without question. Such an unthinking loyalty, when challenged by events, is not, and never can be, held and supported because the very reasons for holding to the approach are neither clear nor arguable. Thus, commitment to a team approach needs to be based upon a clear understanding of the reasons why it is being used, and an acceptance, at least in principle, of the need to abide by the conditions it requires. This has to be learned. As a contractual obligation on the part of the staff it also has to allow for the possibility of challenge, never as an individual or a sub-group rebellion in the form of subverting the accepted practice, but always in terms of discussion within the staff group. Unity with flexibility ensures the ability to adjust to meet altered conditions without destroying the overall pattern.

It is interesting to note that the main perception residents have of approaches where disagreement and disunity amongst staff members surface is that the whole approach is some form of confidence trick. For instance, any treatment programme can only work well if everyone involved, whatever his or her private thoughts, abides by the process as instigated. If consistency (i.e. predictability) or response is one of the main contributions to the establishment of security, then conversely unpredictability must serve to maintain a large element of fear and risk and so of minimizing the possibility of growth and change.

This book outlines a team approach from the point of view of a psychologist and a psychiatrist involved in a residential setting with disturbed children. Collins and Bruce show how their approach has been used, but more importantly they show how it is created and how a training programme to maintain it can be designed. Inevitably the achievement of cohesion is less than perfect even when all the members of a residential unit team understand fairly clearly what the basic elements of the approach are and even when they have gone through a training programme that involves exercises in team building.

Many of the problems and some of the possible solutions of working with children in restricted space and in a residential setting are highlighted here. Often in such settings personal relationships become a distinct problem especially if the support systems necessarily built into the kind of approach outlined here are ignored or bypassed. The intensity of stress and emotional experience in this very onerous and difficult work can seldom be absorbed by the individual without costs that usually impair efficient practice.

So this book also looks at staff support systems, ways in which people can create situations and groups that help to relieve the stress of attempting to cope with this kind of work. Support systems have benefits in many directions, not least in improved performance and an increase in job satisfaction for staff, but more importantly in that such systems reduce the risk that staff stress will be 'laid-off' on the residents. As this 'laying-off' process is seldom known to the people who are doing it, and tends to result in impulsive or defensive behaviours, the cost to the efficient functioning of a treatment unit can be very high. Drawing on their experiences, Collins and Bruce have tried to explain the ways in which positive preventive measures can be built into the organizational structure to reduce this resource-drain.

Residential institutions are of many kinds and although all have certain things in common in terms of what they offer, some factors are essentially different, for example directed to different or more specific aims, or more concentrated. Collins and Bruce are writing about residential units with treatment orientation where the emphasis is on personal growth as well as containment and behavioural change. It needs to be stressed that even in residential units where treatment has not such a specific focus nor such a primary aim, knowledge of the ways in which treatment can be applied can have great bearing upon the daily functioning of that unit. For instance, the maintenance of 'law and order' in a treatment-oriented unit has implications for any residential situation.

'Group living' is a concept applicable to all forms of residential care, but when groups as elements of treatment are used within the overall 'living' situation, problems of the inclusion or exclusion of élites and rejects become hugely important. The difference is simply one of degree. Exactly these kinds of problems are to be found in all residential units, the difference being that because the structures that bring them into existence are less formalized, the consequences are less easily attributable to the causes. It is suggested here that residential workers from different professional backgrounds can all be regarded as group workers and that such an all-embracing term could go a long way to mitigating professional rivalry and also to forming a central core of discipline to which few might object. Few, too, would see it as a threat to their professional integrity.

Finally, this book offers some insight for residential workers into the nature of 'being part of an organization'. By this I mean that many members of the helping professions tend to stress their individuality, usually in terms of their professional responsibility, to the point where they see the organization in which they work as relatively incidental to their practice. Collins and Bruce show quite clearly that this perception has possibly dangerous consequences. They stress that a full understanding of the organization is essential if maximum use for beneficial ends is to be made of all the resources available. After all, organizations are created to support and facilitate as well as to confine, though it is often only the latter that becomes apparent.

TOM DOUGLAS
February 1983

Preface

For many years the authors of this book have acted as consultants to institutions in which disturbed adolescents are treated. In very many of these institutions the authors have found that the staff, often very young themselves, are expected to deal with considerable degrees of disturbance in the young people in their care. In the authors' experience, however, it is the exception rather than the rule that the staff in adolescent institutions have been provided with systematic information about how to undertake their therapeutic tasks. This book is offered in the hope that it will provide a starting point for staff and for those who are responsible for their training to begin to think systematically about acquiring a body of knowledge and a set of skills to equip them for their tasks.

The book starts with an account of some current notions about the nature of adolescence. The rest of the book is divided into two parts. The first concentrates on the impact that disturbed adolescents can have upon staff and looks at various ways in which staff can divert the energies and emotions of disturbed adolescents into fruitful growth. The second part is devoted to the concept of developing effective team work. This is especially important in work with adolescents who, as a group, are remarkably adept at creating difficulties and causing distress amongst those who are trying to help them. The book finishes with a brief postscript about secure units. There is considerable controversy about the need for such units for adolescents and this is an area where our ignorance can all too frequently be masked by misconceptions.

The contents of this book represent the authors' views alone and in no way commit the Department of Health and Social Security.

1 Adolescence: An Overview

This chapter reviews the course of normal adolescence together with some of its most common aberrations. In addition, some of the main theories that have been advanced to help explain the phenomena observed in adolescence will be outlined. In my experience, a surprising number of very experienced residential social workers have had little in the way of formal training designed to help them understand the nature of adolescence. Indeed, I have heard it argued by a number of people who have had the responsibility for administering adolescent institutions that it is a mistake to burden staff with too much formal teaching. They point out that what disturbed people need more than anything else is people who are able to give them the love and security that have as a rule been lacking in their lives. According to this view, what disturbed adolescents most need are people who have had experience of bringing up their own families and who are, therefore, familiar with the ways of young people.

Unfortunately, in our experience, bringing up one's own adolescent children is not in itself a useful enough experience to equip one to work with disturbed adolescents. Indeed, it can be downright misleading. A middle-aged woman, a mother with several children of her own, had responsibility for a very disturbed boy in a secure institution for adolescents. Very shortly after the boy's admission to the institution his worker was tucking him into bed and was going to bend down to kiss him goodnight when he suddenly hit her full in the mouth. She was not badly hurt physically, but her feelings were desperately hurt and she was left utterly bewildered. For a time she thought about giving up her social work. All her previous experience of her own children had not prepared her for this particular boy's reaction to physical and emotional closeness. She would have been better prepared and more wary if she had had some training in normal and abnormal adolescent development. 'All our knowledge,' as T.S. Eliot pointed out, 'brings us nearer to our ignorance' (Eliot 1963 : 161).

The physical and emotional changes of adolescence are the result of chemical changes in the child's body. The main chemicals involved are the hormones. These are chemical messengers produced by small but extremely potent glands in the brain. One of the triggers for puberty seems to be a lowering of the amount of a particular hormone called melatonin. Melatonin is produced in the pineal gland at the top of the brain. The pineal gland was originally thought, for example by Descartes, to be the seat of the soul. It is a vestigeal third eye and it may be responsive to the number of day/night cycles that are passed in an individual's life. It has been found that rabbits that have been brought up in darkness have delayed puberty. It may be, therefore, that under normal circumstances puberty does not start until the child has gone through a minimum number of day/night cycles. Perhaps this is a safeguard to ensure that puberty does not start too early. Melatonin has a lightening effect on the skin and as its level falls, the skin and hair become darker. This is the reason why young children have a tendency to be fair, but become darker as they get older. As the level of melatonin drops in the blood, the pituitary gland at the base of the brain is switched on and starts to produce hormones called gonadotrophins. (The gonads are the testis and ovary; gonadotrophin literally means gonad feeders.) The latter travel through the bloodstream and cause the testis in the male and the ovary in the female to enlarge and to start to produce sperms and ova. The testis and ovary are themselves glands and the male and female hormones they produce are responsible for the development of adult sex characteristics, i.e. in the male, beard development, deepening of the voice, enlargement of the penis, and increased muscle development. In the female, the ovary hormones induce breast development, redistribution of body fat to give a more feminine figure, and the development of underarm and pubic hair. In both boys and girls the hormonal changes also cause a growth spurt.

The production of gonadotrophins is very sensitive to body weight. If the body weight falls below a certain level, gonadotrophin production is reduced and the changes of puberty are halted or reversed. Adolescents who are suffering from anorexia nervosa probably have as their unconscious aim the reduction of weight to a point where they return to a pre-pubertal state in order not to have to face the emotional demands of adolescent sexuality.

Theories of the nature of adolescence have had a tendency to precede detailed observation of normal adolescence. Many of the theories have been based on work with disturbed young people and this has certainly skewed our view of what normal adolescence is like. One of the commonly held views of adolescence is that it is necessarily a period of alienation from parents and from adult values. The experience of alienation was very vividly put to us by a fourteen-year-old girl who said that she felt utterly isolated in her family. She had no sense of belonging to her parents or to her older sister. She literally described them as being alien to her. It was as though they had come from a different planet. She could not use them in any way to help her. This girl, however, suffered from severe problems in addition to her feeling of alienation.

A more common form of experience for young people is the conviction that they must be adopted, because their parents seem so strange to them. Is it in fact true, however, that all adolescents go through a period of alienation? Douvan and Adelson (1966), who interviewed 3000 adolescents, found that although there were disagreements between young people and their parents over relatively minor issues such as type of music preferred, the suitability of friends, and modes of dressing, there was nevertheless a remarkable degree of concord between young people and their parents over major issues such as religion and sexual attitudes. On the whole, most of the young people got on fairly well with their parents despite occasional disagreements.

It also seems to be a mistake to assume that young people are in general 'anti-authority'. John Coleman (1980) has reported that when young people in London's East End schools were asked about their teachers they said that some of them behaved as though they were frightened of the children. On the whole they preferred teachers who could keep order and who had some degree of authority over a class. This adolescent respect for authority (and disillusionment when it failed) was well described by Erich Maria von Remarque (1963) in his book *All Quiet on the Western Front*:

> 'For us lads of 18, they [the adults] ought to have been medi-ators and guides to the world of maturity, the world of work, of duty, of culture, of progress – to the future. We often made fun of them and played jokes on them, but in our hearts we trusted them. The idea of authority which they repre-sented was associated in our minds with a greater insight and a more humane wisdom, but the first death we saw shattered this belief. We had to recognise that our generation was more to be trusted than theirs. They surpassed us only in phrases and cleverness. The first bombardment showed us our mistake and under it the world as they had taught it to us, broke in pieces.' (von Remarque 1963 : 14)

Related to the idea of alienation is the notion that adolescence is characteristically a time of stress, the so-called Sturm and Drang theory. The 'crazy mixed-up kid' is a stereotype familiar to us all and is well portrayed in books such as Salinger's *Catcher in the Rye* (1951) and Philip Roth's *Portnoy's Complaint* (1971). Most psychoanalytical writers certainly view adolescence as a period of particular difficulty. However, this may be a distorted view because, on the whole, analysts work with disturbed young people. Graham and Rutter (1973) conducted a study in the Isle of Wight of the rates of psychiatric disorder in children and adolescents. They found that in the Isle of Wight approximately 13 per cent of fourteen-year-olds were suffering from significant psychiatric disorder. This figure was arrived at on the basis of questionnaires filled out by teachers and parents. If, however, young people were questioned directly about experiences of unhappiness, the figure rose from 13 to 21 per cent. These figures would certainly be higher in inner-city areas.

The figure of 21 per cent would certainly give some credence to the idea of adolescence being a period of storm and stress, but it still leaves approximately 80 per cent of young people in the Isle of Wight who are not suffering from psychiatric disorder. The difficulty about notions such as storm and stress is that they are very difficult to quantify. Certainly, however, as adolescence advances, there is a change in the pattern of psychiatric disorder. There is a relative increase in the number of girls suffering from such disorder. Boys out-number girls in referral to child guidance clinics at the age of eight years, but as adolescence proceeds the girls start to overtake the boys. In addition, depression, anxiety, and psychotic illness such as schizophrenia and manic depressive illness increase, and in general there is a shift towards a more adult pattern of psychiatric disorder. In our experience, however, disturbed adolescents can demonstrate a bewildering variety of symptoms that may shift almost from day to day. Diagnosis in this age group can therefore be difficult. In particular, there is a tendency to over-diagnose schizophrenia unless very strict diagnostic criteria are adhered to. Disturbed adolescents can often present with bizarre and histrionic symptoms: for example, a fifteen-year-old patient of ours believed that she was the reincarnation of an Egyptian mummified cat. This symptom cleared up very rapidly, however, when attention was paid to the marital difficulties being experienced by her parents.

Another very marked change in adolescence is the appearance of suicidal behaviour. The ratio of suicidal and attempted suicidal behaviour in pre-pubertal children is extremely low. With the onset of adolescence, however, self-destructive behaviour increases. There is a sex difference: boys are relatively more vulnerable to actually killing themselves; girls are more prone to attempted suicide (acts such as wrist-slashing and pill-taking), often in a rather histrionic way. Girls are also prone to outbreaks of imitative self-destructive behaviour especially in institutions. In one institution, for example, there was an outbreak of the swallowing of open safety pins and in another of friction-burning with blankets. These outbreaks tend to die down as quickly as they arise. There is some evidence (see, for example, Shaffer 1979) to show that young people who succeed in killing themselves are of relatively superior intelligence and often also tall for their age. It is worth bearing the latter in mind because while from an adult point of view it may seem a good thing that a young person should be bigger than his or her peers, the adolescent may feel quite differently. We were extremely concerned when a thirteen-year-old boy who was six feet four inches tall disappeared for twenty-four hours after climbing out of his bedroom. He had felt very isolated and bewildered in school and far from being proud of his height thought of it as being monstrous.

The question of para-suicide raises the issue of giving drugs to adolescents. Experience has taught us never to leave an adolescent in charge of his or her own medication. As a rule, disturbed adolescents tend to be forgetful of their medication, but then tend to take their pills by the handful when they are feeling depressed. They also have a tendency to swap pills with their friends.

Adolescence is a period of group or gang formation and a period of identification with particular causes, be it nuclear disarmament, punk rock, or some other subcultural style. A number of theories have been advanced to explain the emotional investment of young people in gangs and causes and these will be reviewed when we look at the ideas of Anna Freud and Erik Erikson. Not all adolescent gangs are delinquent, but certainly young people in a group have a tendency to egg each other on to delinquent acts that they might not indulge in if alone. Indeed, the peak rate for delinquency is at the ages of fifteen and sixteen. As Donald West (1967) in *The Young Offender* has written, juvenile delinquency is 'like an attack of the measles, a first conviction in a schoolboy, though it can be serious, does not usually portend a blighted future', and it does not usually mean that the young person is destined for a life of crime. Most juvenile delinquency in this country is dishonest crime, i.e. thieving. There seems no doubt, however, that recently there has been a definite increase in the rate of violent crime and also an increase in the ratio of girls to boys involved in delinquency. There certainly seems to be an increasing tendency for girls to indulge in violence (Rutter 1979 : 122).

Adolescence is often associated in the popular mind with drink, drugs, and sex. Adolescents are more vulnerable to peer group pressures and so it is not surprising that many young people have at one time or another experimented with taking the odd pill or a sniff of glue. Usually, however, such behaviour is an attempt to 'stay in' with the group and only a small minority of such young people progress to being habitual drug users. In our experience, young people who are particularly vulnerable to the latter tend to be loners who have no firm friends and who tend to use drugs either as a way of making themselves feel more confident or to blot out anxiety. Very rapidly their significant relationship becomes one with the drug rather than with people. As to the use of alcohol, there seems to be no doubt that young people are drinking more and that they are doing so in relatively greater numbers than the adult population (Rutter 1979 : 138).

The notion that young people are particularly sexually promiscuous is probably unfounded. Inasmuch as they are promiscuous, they probably reflect changes in sexual habits in society as a whole. In our experience many disturbed adolescents are more comfortable in talking about sex than in actually indulging in it. As one sixteen-year-old boy confided after he had intercourse with his girlfriend, 'I did not really like it, I would much rather have listened to my record player'. Doctors and residential staff themselves are often faced with the painful question 'should this young girl be on a contraceptive pill or not?'. This is an issue that staff can feel very disturbed about and questions of religious belief and moral conviction may be involved. Whilst clearly every case has to be judged on its individual merits, it has been our experience (at least with disturbed adolescents) that if they are sexually promiscuous they are also promiscuous about taking contraceptive pills. They cannot be trusted to take the medication regularly and so residential staff may find themselves in the position of having to give out the pills even though they feel that what they are doing is wrong. Some girls do not take their contraceptive pills because they actually want to have a baby. Deprived girls quite commonly have the fantasy that if they have a baby of their own it will provide them with the love that they feel they have missed out on in their earlier years.

At this point it will be useful to review the ideas of some of the theoreticians of adolescence.

MOSES LAUFER

Moses Laufer is a psychoanalyst who helped found the Brent Consultation Centre (an adolescent walk-in service) in North West London. Laufer's central theory of adolescence is quite a simple one. He believes that the main task that adolescents face is coming to terms with their changing bodies. Parents tend to remember rather little about the painfulness of the physical change in their adolescent years, but for many adolescents the changing of their body and the onset of adult sexual feelings can be very frightening. The extent to which such feelings can become integrated into the total personality will depend upon the adolescent's past experience and upon his or her present circumstances.

Roy, a seventeen-year-old, was referred to us because of insomnia. For about six months before we met Roy he had been waking in the middle of the night and could not get back to sleep again until just before getting up. Throughout the day he felt moody and irritable. He was an only child and his parents had split up when he was three years old. His father made very little attempt to keep in touch with Roy and this left him feeling angry and hurt, although he put up a pretence of saying that his father meant nothing to him. Roy and his mother had always been very close, but she had been prone to depression and to a number of physical illnesses. She was, in fact, very ill for the first six months of Roy's life. In discussion with Roy it soon became clear that he had great difficulty in accepting the development of his adult sexuality. Although he was interested in girls he was frightened of having a close relationship with one. He was lying awake at night and struggling to keep sexual thoughts and fantasies at bay and felt that if he relaxed into sleep they would take control of him. His difficulty in coming to terms with his adult sexuality was clearly related to his wish not to identify with an adult male (his disappointing and hurtful father) and to his fear that his over-close relationship with his mother would spill over into an adult sexual one.

According to Laufer's view, many of the attacks that young people make upon their own bodies are an attempt to control them. Similarly, some young people will deliberately court getting cold, going out with flimsy clothing on almost as though literally to dampen down the fires of sexual ardour. One boy we know, who had been admitted to a secure unit for arson offences, was for a time unable to bear any sort of warmth. The radiator in his room had always to be turned off and he would even sit beside an open refrigerator.

ANNA FREUD

Anna Freud's model of adolescence has much in common with her father Sigmund Freud's model of mourning. According to Anna Freud, adolescents have the difficult task of withdrawing their emotional energy (in psychoanalytic terms, libido) from their parents and eventually reinvesting it in a peer of the opposite sex. Rather like mourning, this is not a process that can occur overnight and many of the phenomena of adolescence can be understood in terms of the vicissitudes of the withdrawn libido. The feeling of alienation and the bleakness of adolescence may be understood because the young person's emotional energy, although withdrawn from parents, still has not yet found another person to reinvest in. A temporary solution is found if the emotional energy can be put into a gang or an adolescent cause (as indicated above (p. 6), something like nuclear disarmament or a particular religious group, or into being a punk rocker or a skinhead). At times the emotional energy may be diverted back entirely on to the adolescent. At times this can lead to adolescents being very selfish, although if their libido can be channelled partly into a cause they are also capable of remarkable altruism. Occasionally the emotional energy can swing wildly between the self and the parents. One mother found herself quite bewildered because for much of the time her adolescent daughter treated her like dirt. The situation could switch rapidly to the daughter sitting on her knee or even getting into bed with her to have a cuddle.

According to this model of adolescence there inevitably must be some difficulty in the adolescent years as the emotional energy is put first into one and then into another person or cause.

ERIK ERIKSON

Erik Erikson, like Anna Freud and Moses Laufer, is a psycho-analyst. However, his theory of adolescence is somewhat differ-ent in that he tends to stress the importance of the adolescent in relation to society rather than thinking of adolescent problems as being rooted mainly in changes within the adolescent. Erikson sees the acquiring of an adult identity as the main task of adoles-cence. He considers this to be a formidable task because it means the difference between a twelve-year-old who has just started at a secondary school and an eighteen-year-old who may be about to go to university, or to get married, or who may actually be a parent.

For Erikson, identity is a combination of two needs. First, a feeling within the adolescent that he or she has a place in society, and, second, the recognition and reinforcement by society through its allocation of roles to the adolescent. In primitive societies such allocation of roles is highly ritualized and there is not much leeway for the adolescent to step outside the assigned roles. Modern Western societies allow their young people much more in the way of choice of roles and the richer societies even allow what Erikson calls a psycho-social moratorium, i.e. a period when the adolescents can, in effect, drift without having to fit into any particular role. Erikson himself had such a mora-torium. When he was an adolescent he wandered around Europe with no particular goal in mind.

The relative lack of role definition in modern Western socie-ties can, however, put a considerable strain on some adoles-cents, particularly those in whom the foundations of identity are shaky because of poor childhood experiences. Adopted children can also experience confusion with their identity because they feel cut off from their roots. Erikson (1968) describes adolescents who are having difficulties in accomplishing an adult identity as suffering from identity diffusion or from role confusion. Such young people may opt for a negative identity in order to reduce their confusion. By negative identity, Erikson means reversal of adult and particularly parental values and expectations. For example, a very confused and unhappy fourteen-year-old Jewish girl from a very religious family deliberately set out to belittle Jewish institutions and would make a point of defiling her parents' cooking vessels by cooking such things as pork sausages in them. Adolescents may also seek to reduce their identity diffusion by what Erikson has called 'identity foreclosure' in which the young person tries to adopt a role before they are emotionally able to integrate it into their personality. Some teenage marriages are of this sort and very frequently turn out badly.

There is a particular trap for academically gifted children in our society who may find themselves channelled through 'O' and 'A' levels and into university or technical college without really feeling that they have had much say in the matter. Such young people may break down at university or switch courses in an attempt to feel that there is something of them in what they are doing.

DAVID ELKIND

David Elkind's (1967) review of adolescence emphasizes the particular way in which adolescents think as compared with children and adults. Elkind believes that a good deal of adolescent disturbance can be understood in terms of a young person's struggle to come to terms with abstract thinking. As they move from the egocentric mode of thinking of the small child (events in the outside world are related to the self – e.g. parental quarrels are thought to be the result of something that they, the child, has done wrong) to a mode of thinking in which they come to realize that the individual human being is simply part of a multi-generational cycle of birth, life, and death, a sense of confusion, at times even amounting to depersonalization, may result. An adolescent's espousal of particular causes may be seen as an attempt to try to regain some control over the outside world. This shift in mode of thinking can be particularly difficult for those adolescents who as children did not have enough of a sense of being able to effect changes in their family environment according to their needs.

JOHN COLEMAN

John Coleman, who was Senior Lecturer in Psychology at the London Hospital Medical College, has put forward what he calls a 'focal theory' of adolescence. Coleman thinks of adolescence as representing a period in which a number of adolescent maturational tasks or issues have to be coped with (such as anxiety over heterosexual relationships and fears of rejection from peer group). He believes that concerns about different issues reach a peak at different stages in the adolescent process. In other words, adolescents cope with the various tasks facing them by spreading the process over a number of years and tackling one particular issue at a time (although, of course, there is usually a certain amount of overlap). As in the case of late developers, difficulties arise when puberty and the growth spurt coincide with other pressures such as conflicts with parents and teachers.

DONALD WINNICOTT

Donald Winnicott's (1971) contribution to the understanding of adolescence is an emphasis on the healthy aspect of assertive or even possibly aggressive behaviour. At every stage in his or her development, the child needs to be able to assert his or her own identity in the face of powerful parents. For example, the baby must feel free to demand food and to make hungry attacks on the breast or bottle. The toddler must feel free to say 'no' and, if necessary, to have a temper tantrum. The primary-school child must feel able to assert his or her own independence enough to prefer being at school or out playing with friends rather than always being at home. The adolescent has to feel able to challenge, if necessary in a positively aggressive way, the beliefs and opinions of the adults who are responsible for him or her. If all goes well in a child's development then this assertiveness can be achieved without leading to a disruption of the bond between parents and child. The love in the relationship is enough to outlive the inevitable arguments and hatreds of the family life. However, where an adolescent has had a previous experience of parenting where he or she has not felt safe to be assertive – for example, where a parent has been absent, or has been mentally or physically ill, or perhaps has even died – ordinary assertiveness can take on a frightening quality. Such adolescents find themselves in the position of someone who is frightened of heights and yet who knows that he or she must climb down a cliff. In order to get the experience over with, the person may hurry or even hurl themselves down. Adolescents who are the most unsure about their aggressiveness may need to attack the grown-ups who are responsible for them again and again in order to reassure themselves that the grown-ups have survived. For example, a fifteen-year-old boy presented with behaviour that was very frightening to his parents. Although most of the time he was very considerate to his father (who was in a wheel chair and who suffered from disseminated sclerosis), he tended to stay out late at night. He could suddenly flare up and on one occasion was found hurling milk bottles at the front door. This boy had an older sister who had left the family some years before and was bringing up a family of her own and so was unable to lend support. His mother was chronically depressed as a result of worrying about her husband's illness. The boy was clearly terrified of the effect that his adolescent assertiveness was having upon his parents. Some of the time he managed to cope by looking after his father's needs and so being a good son, but on occasion his terror and rage spilled out in his aggressive acts. In the end he had to go into a community school where he was able to settle because he had grown-ups around him who could take the strain; at the same time his parents received social work support.

According to Winnicott, normal adolescence always involves the fantasy of aggressively attacking and replacing the parents but with the proviso that this should be a 'game'. As indicated above (p. 13), if the parents die or become ill in any way, or if they leave the adolescent, the 'game' ceases and the adolescent finds him- or herself in difficulties.

CONCLUSION

Human behaviour is so complex that no single theory can be expected to cover all aspects of it. The behaviour of adolescents is no exception to this rule and so those who work with adolescents need a series of different models to refer to in trying to understand the behaviour of the young people they are trying to help. The models outlined above are, we believe, the main ones currently in use in this country.

2 The Role of the Residential Worker

Even when armed with a knowledge of the nature of adolescence and its main abnormalities, working with disturbed adolescents can be a profoundly upsetting and confusing experience. In this chapter we shall be looking at the main functions of workers with disturbed adolescents and at the difficulties presented by these functions. We shall also be considering some of the risks that such workers face and shall be mentioning some ways in which the risks can be reduced.

Arthur Hyatt-Williams (1971) has described three main functions of the worker with adolescents: (1) the worker as caregiver; (2) the worker as custodian and limit-setter; and (3) the worker as therapist.

(1) THE RESIDENTIAL WORKER AS CAREGIVER

The residential social worker is clearly *in loco parentis* to the adolescents in his or her charge. The social worker has to be prepared to provide the love and care that all children, and indeed adults to a lesser extent, need in order to develop their personalities to the full. At times this will involve the worker tending to the adolescents' most intimate bodily needs. Such work is difficult. Although adolescents may be in desperate need of such care, they will not be able to accept it easily because of their need to begin to develop an identity of their own. The residential social worker will, therefore, have to recognize the adolescent's need for intimate contact whilst at the same time respecting the distance that the adolescent (particularly the disturbed adolescent) needs to maintain between him- or herself and those looking after him or her.

An example of residential social work at its best will illustrate this point. A worker looking after a fourteen-year-old boy noted that the boy was in the habit of wetting his bed. The worker mentioned this in a very business-like manner to the boy in private and they set up a routine whereby if an accident had occurred the boy would leave his sheets by the bed and the worker would replace them with clean sheets whilst all the children were down at breakfast. It was left to the boy to make up his bed with the sheets. No more was said about the matter and as the routine established itself the rate of bed-wetting decreased considerably. The worker had succeeded in respecting the boy's desire to begin to take charge of his own body whilst at the same time acknowledging a childish need.

The ability to provide adolescents with what they need is based upon the ability to put oneself in their shoes. If this process of identification can continue alongside the ability to distinguish between what it is that the adolescent needs and what it is that is being brought from the adolescent worker's own experience, all is well. In residential social work, however, one frequently sees examples of over- and under-identification with adolescents. These are actually different expressions of the same phenomenon. Few of us have had a perfectly satisfying experience of childhood and so each of us brings areas of privation and of deprivation to our work with young people. In many ways this is a good thing because it is the driving force that adds momentum to our work and keeps us going through periods of difficulties with the young people we are looking after. If a worker has known a young person for some time, a bond can develop between them which at times can take on an almost uncanny quality. Hyatt-Williams (1971) writes about a boy whom he had in psychotherapy. One day the boy missed his usual session. That night Hyatt-Williams had a dream in which he saw the boy with a detailed dissection of the armpit. A few days later Hyatt-Williams heard that the boy had killed himself. Another example is that of a residential social worker who was taking a holiday at home. On one of the days of his holiday he felt impelled to light a fire in his garden and as he was doing so he felt certain that there was something wrong with the boy in his charge. In fact on that very day the boy had broken into a shop and had attacked three policemen. Presumably both Hyatt-Williams and the residential social worker were responding to sub-conscious cues from the children in their charge.

On occasion, parents similarly will develop a pain or will hurt themselves in the same part of their body where their child has been injured. Similar phenomena can occur between residential social workers and the children they are looking after. A fifteen-year-old girl was deliberately badly scalded on the foot by some young men who were harbouring her when she ran away from an institution. A few days after the girl's return her residential social worker accidentally scalded her own foot. When this incident was discussed it became clear that the residential social worker had felt (in fact quite unjustifiably) extremely guilty about the girl absconding from the unit and just like a parent who had felt she had let her child down, attacked herself, in this case not only emotionally, but also physically.

The above are not uncommon examples of identification. Occasionally, however, particularly where staff have had very depriving experiences as children, or where they are currently going through a very difficult period in their own lives, they will identify with the children in their care to such an extent that their judgement is impaired. For example, a sensitive and intelligent man was appointed to be the Head of a unit in a large institution. He had no previous experience of residential work. He was appointed to his relatively high position because he had done so well in his previous post (which was in the nature of a research project). He was very devoted to his work and soon came to identify strongly with the children in his charge. He felt very keenly that there had been too much emphasis on the custodial side of the work in the institution and he wanted to introduce a more therapeutic element. When, for example, one of the boys drew graffiti over the walls of his room he discussed the symbolism of this with the boy, but did not tell the boy to wipe the graffiti off the wall. He soon came to feel that the magistrates who committed children to the institution were biased and that in making such decisions they were bolstering a society that was itself creating delinquency in children. Although on the whole the children in his care liked him, the number of absconsions and the amount of vandalism within his unit increased because he felt unable to exert controls that he thought of as being custodial. In the end, after a heated argument with the managers of the institution, he had to leave. This man so identified with the difficulties of the children in his care that he was unable to see them as part of a larger society which itself had needs and that the children themselves needed controls as well as care. Indeed, as we shall see later, where disturbed adolescents are concerned, control is an important aspect of care.

On occasion over-identification with adolescents can assume dangerous proportions. Some residential social workers derive a positive excitement from the delinquency of the young people they are caring for. Under the guise of supporting such young people against the attacks of society, and as a way of getting close to the children, such residential workers may try to abolish the normal boundaries between grown-ups and adolescents and try to relate to the adolescents at their own level. For example, a worker felt that he had a special relationship with the boy in his charge. He felt that the boy was always being picked on by other members of staff and sought to protect him, even to the extent of covering up for him when the boy committed misdemeanours. He and the boy would go on long walks together and the boy would tell him things that apparently he would not tell other members of the staff. Needless to say this particular worker soon found himself quite isolated in relation to his fellow workers and the boy was able to play one staff member off against another because important information about him was being withheld from the general group. In the end, in fact, both the boy and the worker came to be generally disliked. The staff member soon became so isolated that he became suspicious of the motives of his fellow workers and felt they were getting at him. A series of very painful staff meetings went some way to resolving the crisis, but in the end the boy had to be discharged without getting the full benefit of the help the institution could have given him.

It is generally a mistake to feel that one is particularly special to an adolescent in one's charge. Obviously adolescents have clear-cut preferences, but they tend to feel extremely uneasy about special relationships and they can signal such unease by delinquent behaviour. Indeed, when adolescents are behaving badly in an institution it is useful to look first at ways in which staff tensions might be contributing to such behaviour. Many residential social workers quite rightly feel that it is their duty to make up for the lack of love and affection that many of their young people have suffered. It is important to remember, however, that even though a young person has had a life in which consistent love and affection have been absent, the young person may not consciously be aware of this. Indeed, he or she may have developed very tough defences that exclude the possibility of their coming to rely on an adult who may, by letting them down, hurt them very deeply. Perhaps because of emotionally cold experiences in their own childhood, some residential workers have a need to have their love and attention reciprocated by the young people in their care. When the young person appears not to respond they may redouble their efforts in order to make contact. For example, a staff member became very attached to the fifteen-year-old girl in her charge. This particular staff member had had a somewhat unhappy childhood because her own mother had suffered a certain amount of illness and, indeed, was at the time again very unwell. The young girl had also had a poor experience of mothering and became very unhappy and disturbed when her mother failed to turn up for expected visits. The staff member tried to make up for this lack of care from the natural mother but her efforts were rewarded by the girl absconding and getting into a lot of trouble. At this point the staff member severely castigated herself and became very unhappy, even to the point of depression. She felt that she could not stop weeping and required a lot of support from her fellow members of staff. In staff support groups she was able to begin to see that her attempts to help the girl were largely geared to helping herself with her unhappiness about her own mother. It should be pointed out at this stage that whilst such behaviour may be very clear to people observing it, the person 'acting out' their own difficulties through the adolescent is as a rule quite unaware of what they are doing.

At the opposite end of the spectrum is, what we call 'under-identification'. Staff may seek to control their own experiences of childhood deprivation by attacking or trying to deny manifestations of deprivation in the adolescents in their charge. A recently appointed worker in a closed unit for adolescents, who had a lot of experience in comprehensive schools, felt that his fellow workers' continued attempts to understand the delinquent behaviour of the young people in their charge, was just plain silly. He felt, and to some extent was justified in doing so, that the educational needs of the children were being overlooked by the staff. He devised a new way of assessing the children's educational attainments but became disheartened when the children failed to make the educational progress he had wished for. In the end he decided to leave the institution. He tended to blame his fellow workers for not helping him in his project and was unable to appreciate their point of view that he had concentrated exclusively on the educational side in order to avoid experiencing overwhelming feelings stirred up by the very disturbed children in his care.

A final point that should be made in connection with the care-giving aspect of residential care is whether young people should be encouraged to visit the homes of the residential social workers. We do not think that any hard-and-fast rule should be made here. It can be very beneficial to young people and the staff looking after them to meet informally at the staff member's home. It should never be forgotten, however, that staff members' own children can become very jealous of other young people brought into their homes. Certainly, any out-of-hours contact between a residential social worker and young people should be discussed by the staff group and monitored by them very closely. The latter is a useful rule in order to prevent staff splits arising out of a staff member developing a special relationship with an adolescent.

(2) THE RESIDENTIAL WORKER AS CUSTODIAN AND LIMIT-SETTER

It is, of course, an aspect of normal parenting to set limits to children's behaviour both to prevent them from getting into trouble and danger and to show them what is socially acceptable. It goes without saying that residential social workers should make it clear to the young people in their care that socially unacceptable behaviour is not the norm. Unfortunately, a minority of residential social workers have a tendency to regard ordinary day-to-day discipline as being in some ways untherapeutic. This can sometimes be baffling to the adolescents themselves and leave them feeling insecure. Adolescents who have had bad or deficient experiences of parenting do, of course, find it extremely difficult to accept ordinary social norms of behaviour. This should, however, be regarded as a technical problem to be tackled by the staff rather than by abandoning ordinary social demands upon the young people.

In thinking about limit-setting we have found two models of behaviour of particular value. The first derives from Sigmund Freud's (1978) notion of a contact barrier. The infant and small child needs its parents to provide a barrier to stimuli that are potentially overwhelming. Parents feed their small children before the stimulus of hunger can become overwhelming. In addition, the parent will not allow a small child to encounter too many strange people, and will also be there to help the small child to cope with new situations. At the same time as protecting the child, the parent will also be stimulating him or her and helping to provide situations that are exciting and interesting. The parents, and particularly the mother in the early stages of a child's life, provide enough stimulation for their child to develop normally, but prevent the child from being overwhelmed by stimulation before the child is ready to cope with it. In the language of information theory, parents help the child to stay somewhere between information-input overload and information-input underload.

Almost by definition, deprived children have not had an experience of this sort of parenting. As a result, they are usually unable to cope with a wide range of stimulation and information. They tend to be easily distracted, to be poor at taking in new information, and to find social interaction, particularly of an intimate sort, overwhelming. In a recent conversation with a woman in her thirties, who had a very deprived childhood and who had been in a number of different institutions, the woman told us that she found it impossible to live with anyone, including her own children, for any length of time. She soon found that she could not bear the close interaction with them that living under the same roof entailed. The consequence of this inability to handle new information and to tolerate close social relationships is that, paradoxically, deprived young people often find it more comfortable and less demanding to live in a depriving environment. This is, I think, why places such as secure adolescent units, special hospitals, prisons, and psychiatric units have a tendency to become institutionalized. The point about an institutionalized institution is that all the functions of the institution become geared towards soulless routine without an element of human interaction, except of the most perfunctory sort. Institutionalization tends to make for a quieter life for both staff and inmates, but unfortunately it also precludes the possibility of growth.

It is important, however, for staff working with very deprived young people to realize that at first the young person may need a wide emotional distance from staff and a very routine and even stark existence. For example, a boy with a very deprived background always demonstrated that he was finding life overwhelming by turning his room into an impossible tip. He always found relief by having his room stripped to the bare minimum and being put on a very strict routine for a few days. Another boy, an arsonist, demonstrated his inability to form close relationships by an abnormal fondness for cold conditions. He could not tolerate any heating in his room and on days that other people would regard as mild, he would sit in front of a refrigerator with the door open. He felt better when he was given a very strict routine to stick to and, indeed, in the initial stages of his management in the secure institution in which he had been placed, he became extremely disturbed if this routine was broken. He began to think that he could communicate with his dead mother through the record player and he criss-crossed his room with intricate lengths of flex. With these sorts of examples in mind, it is obvious that far from being untherapeutic, routine and discipline are an integral part of the management of disturbed adolescents. Indeed, as Bruggen and Pitt-Aikens (1975) have pointed out, adolescents are often searching for an element of authority, which they have previously missed, in those who are looking after them.

The second model that we have found useful in the management of disturbed adolescents is that of Abraham Maslow (1976 : 365). Maslow has pointed out that human beings have what he called both higher and lower 'order needs'. Lower-order needs have to be met before higher-order needs can be satisfied. Lower-order needs are for the basic requisites of life – food, warmth, and shelter, and for a degree of security and consistency in the environment. Higher-order needs are for experiences such as self-esteem and for what Maslow calls 'self-actualization', that is, a sense of one's self or identity as playing a part in the evolution of society as a whole.

Very deprived young people have usually not had an experience of lower-order needs being met and they need such an experience before they can make use of provision for higher-order needs. Lower-order needs can be met by providing a very consistent environment with well-understood daily routines and clear guidelines to expected behaviour. Very disturbed young people need a physical and social environment that they know can withstand the attacks they make upon it. The most disturbed group will need a building that they cannot easily damage or escape from, and they will need staff who can withstand their physical and emotional attacks without retaliating. We think that secure rooms or padded cells can have a place in the management of extremely disturbed adolescents both because they provide an environment that the adolescent cannot destroy and because they provide a respite for staff that enables them to survive. Having said this, however, whenever staff have had to make a decision to put a disturbed adolescent into a locked room (or to sedate them, as more commonly tends to occur in adolescent psychiatric units), the whole incident should be thoroughly discussed, initially by the staff on their own and then by the staff with the young people, to try to understand how a situation in which the young person had become out of control had been allowed to develop. In general, therefore, the more there is a need to confine and to discipline adolescents, the greater is the need for the unit to function as a therapeutic community. In using the term 'therapeutic community', we are following the definition used by Maxwell Jones (1968). He described such a community as one in which the total resources of the community (that is, everything that happens within it) are used as far as possible towards a therapeutic end. In such a community treatment is not simply thought of in terms of the use of drugs to treat mental illness or of psychotherapeutic sessions, but as being something that is occurring every minute of every day and in every situation. Therapeutic communities are usually characterized by a series of daily meetings in which everything of importance that has occurred during the previous twenty-four hours is carefully examined and its significance discussed.

The therapeutic community approach has been described well by both Maxwell Jones (1968) and David Clark (1974). It is also the system in use at the Henderson Hospital in Surrey. Whilst recognizing the need for discipline, the therapeutic community approach provides a safeguard against staff abuse of power. For example, a very gifted but single-minded Head of a semi-secure unit for adolescents found himself being strongly challenged by a fifteen-year-old boy. The boy took every opportunity to challenge the Head's decisions and was also very threatening in a physical way. The Head could not bear to be challenged in this way and started to mete out quite Draconian punishment to the boy. Fortunately, both in staff and in morning community meetings, other members of staff and the young people themselves were able to point out what was happening. It was decided that the main disciplining of the boy should be left to the women members of staff who felt less threatened by him and with whom he was less provocative. This system gave the two protagonists a breathing space, although in the end the boy did have to leave because of continuing difficulties. The therapeutic community approach in this instance averted a potentially extremely dangerous situation in which either the boy or the Head might have been severely injured.

It should be recognized in every institution that disturbed adolescents can be infuriatingly provocative. They are usually also well able to pick out staff members' weakest points and to play upon them. It is, therefore, very important that staff members are allowed to acknowledge and talk about their angry feelings towards the young people. This should not be regarded as unprofessional. Indeed, psychotherapists use their own feelings towards their patients as a useful guide to what is happening in the psychotherapy. A young, hot-blooded, and inexperienced member of staff in an adolescent psychiatric unit was very easily provoked by young people with whom he tended to trade insults. After every episode in which he had found himself in difficulties, he felt able to discuss his feelings with other members of the staff in the daily staff group and was able to talk about his own very large family of origin. He had been the middle one of nine children and his childhood had been largely one in which he had to scramble for what was going. When he found himself working with young people only a few years younger than himself, he felt unable to keep a distance from them and behaved as he would have done in his own family. After about six months of extremely painful experiences (and after all the young people who had been in the unit when he arrived had left) he was able to assert his authority in a more mature fashion and became one of the most valued members of staff.

On very rare occasions a person who is sadistic in their approach will be found working with adolescents. By sadistic we mean deriving a positive pleasure from inflicting punishments rather than using them as guidelines to behaviour. Such people should not, of course, be working with young people or indeed with anyone over whom they might have power. Such individuals often have a certainty and forcefulness that cows their fellow staff members as well as the young people they are looking after. A strong and observant management committee should, however, be able to weed out such individuals before they can do any lasting harm.

A final point should be made about the custodial role of residential social workers. Although many young people in care behave extremely badly themselves, their impulsive behaviour goes along with a very severe conscience. They constantly watch the behaviour of the people who are looking after them and judge it by the severest standards. They feel extremely let down if the grown-ups who are supposed to be looking after them condone bad behaviour in any way or deviate from the highest standards of behaviour. Obviously staff need to have a social life, but it should be kept away from the institution in which they work. Delinquent young people are particularly astute where sexual misbehaviour is concerned. Indeed, the young people may start behaving in a delinquent fashion quite explicitly in order to draw attention to sexual misbehaviour amongst staff members. In one instance, sexual misbehaviour was proclaimed to the world when the young people wrote extremely offensive slogans naming the parties concerned over the walls of their rooms. However painful it may be, illicit relationships amongst staff members that are spilling over into their work must, if necessary, be talked about in staff support groups.

(3) THE RESIDENTIAL WORKER AS THERAPIST

In this section we shall discuss some of the common difficulties presented to workers when they engage in counselling or psychotherapy with young people. (There are many good introductions to psychotherapeutic techniques and we particularly recommend Anthony Storr's (1979) book on this subject.) We shall be describing some of the common difficulties presented by adolescents who have been taken on for counselling and ways in which the difficulties may be handled by the counsellor. We shall be talking particularly about individual counselling in this section.

Adolescents, as a matter of course, tend to wax hot and cold about counselling. At times, if the worker is lucky, they may seem to value it, and at other times can be utterly contemptuous. With delinquent young people, the counsellor is constantly having to battle with 'the gang under the couch'. In the first place, young people often resort to delinquent behaviour in order to avoid having to face their emotional pain. Since the purpose of counselling is to help them to begin to face such pain, the counsellor will automatically find him- or herself having to fight against the adolescent's delinquent defences. With a disturbed adolescent, the course of counselling never runs smooth. There are always difficulties – often acting out of a delinquent kind – to be encountered and these should be expected. For example, a fifteen-year-old boy in an institution told his residential social worker counsellor that the only time he felt really happy and safe was when he was driving a stolen car. He then felt powerful and absolutely in control. At other times he felt wretched and hopeless. In the course of his work with this boy, the counsellor had to endure several periods of severe acting out in which the boy absconded and stole cars. It can be very difficult under these sort of circumstances to keep hold of the idea that as a counsellor one is doing something useful; frequently, pressure is brought to bear to abandon the counselling and to institute more custodial measures. Clearly, the public have to be protected from outrageously delinquent young people, but it is a mistake to think that delinquency-free institutions are necessarily the most effective ones in terms of allowing the young people in them to develop more mature ways of coping.

We shall now look at some of the common difficulties encountered by counsellors working with young people.

(1) The silent adolescent

Ann Hayman (1965), a psychoanalyst, has made the point that a sense of identity is reinforced by a person's ability to put his or her experiences into words. The corollary to this is that adolescents with severe identity problems are very frequently unable to convey in words their experience to other people. The silent adolescent is not, therefore, necessarily one who is simply being obstructive or resistant to counselling. He or she may simply be unable to find words to talk about him- or herself. The counsellor is then faced with a dilemma. The counsellor and the adolescent can either stick it out without anything very much being said, or the counsellor can switch to some activity that does not require words, for example doing woodwork or teaching the young person to read better. On the whole, we have found the latter to be a mistake. This is not to say that activities are not important, but that once formal counselling is embarked upon it is useful to stick at it, however painful.

A useful compromise, especially with younger adolescents is to engage them in Donald Winnicott's (1971) squiggle game. In this game the counsellor and the young person alternately draw squiggles that are then turned into a picture. It is useful to observe both the style and the content of the young person's drawing. A particularly wild and uncontrollable fourteen-year-old girl, who had been described in her local newspaper as being 'a Bonnie without a Clyde', had a tendency to do drawings that were meticulously executed. Every tiny detail was included. This observation enabled the girl and her counsellor to begin to look at the extent to which she tried to control her environment. Her delinquency was, in fact, an attempt to get the world to fit in absolutely with her needs rather than her feeling helpless in the face of reality. The girl's mother had suddenly left home when the girl was ten years old and shortly afterwards had been admitted to a psychiatric hospital with a manic depressive illness. Sometimes the content of the drawings can reveal ideas that were scarcely conscious to the adolescent before they were put on to paper. A fourteen-year-old boy, who had been adopted at about the age of two, was in an institution because of thieving and because of a bizarre episode in which he had attempted to pose as a doctor. He had gone into the local hospital, had somehow acquired a white coat, and had been able to parade about for some time before someone questioned him. This boy started off by doing a series of drawings in which he clearly saw his counsellor as battering at his defences – a battle-axe was bouncing off a shield, a gun was firing at a dug-out, and a fist was battering at a jaw. Very suddenly, however, his defences collapsed and he did a drawing of a figure wrapped in bandages and hanging in chains. He said he thought it was a mummy. Once when he had been to a museum he had seen a mummy wrapped in bandages just like the one in his drawing. It had frightened him, but he had bought a picture of it at the museum shop and he had put it on his wall at home. From this point he was able to begin to talk about some of his fantasies about his own mummy, i.e. his real mother. He wondered what had happened to her. He had the idea that something dreadful must have happened to make her give him away to someone else. It became clear that he was terrified of his own destructiveness and that his delinquency was in part an attempt to seek both punishment and control.

It can sometimes also be useful to use one of several projective techniques such as the 'make-a-picture-story'. In our experience even older adolescents are prepared to do this if they have a trusting relationship with the counsellor. In the make-a-picture-story technique, there are a number of different scenes on to which the young person has to put cut-out figures as though setting up a stage scene. There is a wide range of figures and scenes to choose from. These scenes, and the stories related to them, can often be very revealing. For example, a boy who had been put into an institution because of making several knife attacks had very great difficulty in talking about himself. He was, however, very well able to do the make-a-picture-story. He used two scenes: one of a graveyard, and the other of a desert. In the graveyard scene two people, one of whom was a boy, were burying some treasure they had stolen. The older person in this story suddenly noticed that his wife was buried in the graveyard and told the boy that he could not possibly bury the treasure there. This made the boy angry and he stabbed the older man and took all the treasure for himself. In the desert scene, there was once more a boy and an older man. They had run out of water and the man had been injured. As he was lying on the ground, the boy stabbed him and took all the water for himself. After the boy had done these pictures, the counsellor tried to relate them to the boy's own experiences. The boy was unable to see that the scenes he had depicted had any relevance to his own behaviour. He demonstrated a degree of detachment from his own fantasy world and from his own feelings of remorse which he found extremely frightening. The boy was, however, able to begin to look at his resentment towards his father, who had died when he was four, and towards his stepfather, whom he felt had taken his mother away from him.

Silence in adolescents often indicates extreme suspicion of the counsellor. It is important for adults to remember that adolescents are capable of endowing adults with disproportionate powers and percipience. On occasion, the most innocent remarks can be interpreted by the adolescent as indicating that the counsellor has been able to see right inside the adolescent's mind. Some years after he had been in group psychotherapy, a young man came back to see the group therapist. Half-way through the meeting he began to look puzzled and said 'You know, it is really strange – you don't seem so frightening to me now. I used to think you could read my mind, that you were a real dragon'. It can be useful in therapy with adolescents to bring into the open the fear that many adolescents have that they are going mad and that this will be obvious to the therapist. It is also important to remember that the ability to work with abstract concepts is as yet not complete in adolescents. They have a tendency to take everything literally rather than being able to see that words are only symbols of communication. A sixteen-year-old boy in the middle of a psychotherapy session complained that the therapist was hurling words at him like 'missiles'. The therapist's attempts to point out some of the ways in which the adolescent dealt with his difficulties were experienced as blows directed at him rather than as useful concepts to be played around with.

On occasion, an adolescent will say that he or she could talk more easily with a therapist of the opposite sex. Whilst not dismissing the idea that some therapists and patients are better matched than others, the plea for a member of the opposite sex as a therapist is, in our experience, usually a way of avoiding looking at difficulties and swapping psychotherapists is usually quite unhelpful.

(2) The frightening adolescent

It is not commonly enough recognized, especially by administrators, that working with disturbed adolescents can be a most frightening as well as a most satisfying experience. On occasion, when a unit is going through a difficult period, staff have to summon up considerable courage before they can face coming on duty. Some adolescents radiate menace and this can be particularly off-putting for a worker trying to engage them in therapy. If a worker finds a particular adolescent frightening, it is useful to share this experience with fellow workers to check whether the experience is idiosyncratic or whether it is shared by other people with whom the adolescent comes into contact. If the experience of menace is not generally shared, this usually means that it is some impulse within the worker that is frightening and that he or she is seeing in the adolescent.

It is useful to remember that frightening young people are usually also frightened young people. It is important, initially at least, for a social worker to establish some physical and psychological distance. There is frequently a homosexual element to a young person's fear of the therapist. For example, a seventeen-year-old boy had been behaving very badly and was being taken to his room by his therapist. On the way to the room the therapist gently put his hand on the boy's shoulder. The boy froze and it seemed that he was about to hit the therapist. Instead, he shouted 'Get off you queer' and ran into his room and slammed the door. With such young people it can be useful to sit quite a long way away when talking with them. Sometimes the adolescent will arrange this for a number of sessions until he or she gets used to the therapist. One sixteen-year-old boy, for example, would stand in the middle of the room as though he wanted a head start if he needed to bolt out of the door. In addition to physical distance it can be useful for the therapist to use distancing statements. Rather than being dogmatic, he or she might preface remarks with such phrases as 'I wonder if', or 'It's possible that', or 'Some young people in your position might', and so on.

On occasion some young people, far from being reassured by the therapist keeping a distance, actually seek a physical confrontation in order to gain reassurance and to feel that they can be controlled. In the middle of the night a male therapist was called to see a fourteen-year-old boy whom he had been working with for some time. Two women were on night duty and had been so frightened by the boy's behaviour that they had shut themselves in the unit's sitting room. When the therapist entered the boy's dormitory he found him pacing up and down with a menacing and yet frightened expression on his face. The therapist made it clear to the boy that he was not going to go away until the boy had returned to his bed and calmed down. If necessary, the therapist would stay there all night. When it became clear that the therapist was prepared if necessary to hold the boy down all night, the boy was able to calm himself and return to bed.

On occasion, of course, situations that are downright dangerous will occur in even the best-run adolescent units. Such situations usually arise extremely rapidly and it has to be left to the discretion of the individual workers how to handle them. For example, quite suddenly and unexpectedly a residential social worker who was counselling a girl found himself facing the point of a knife which she had brought into the session. He simply asked her to hand the knife over to him and fortunately she did so. In this case he relied upon his intuition and his previous relationship with the girl. Where there is any doubt in a situation like this, however, the therapist should always play safe and withdraw to get some help. Under no circumstances is it helpful to an adolescent to be able to actually attack or injure the therapist.

A particular source of difficulty is the adolescent who has committed a murder. On the whole, such adolescents are usually only encountered in secure institutions but even the most experienced staff can find such young people extremely disturbing to work with. It is as well for residential social workers to face the fact that murder is something about which it is impossible to be truly dispassionate. Indeed, it is probably a mistake to try to be so. It is interesting to observe different ways in which different staff members cope with their feelings about young murderers. Some workers in our experience actually minimize the fact of the child having murdered even to the extent of not reading the details of the crime in the child's notes. Such workers tend to try to emphasize the child's normality and concentrate on working towards getting the child reintegrated into society. They may, for example, push the authorities to allow the child more in the way of supervised access to outside events. Other staff members may find themselves caught up in the details of the crime and find it impossible to view the child without a feeling of horror. In a staff support group one residential social worker confided that she always found herself looking at a fourteen-year-old boy murderer's hands and thinking of what they had done.

Other workers, in order to control their horror, may try to 'get through' to the adolescent. This is a situation that has to be watched very carefully. Adolescents who have murdered can for much of the time behave perfectly normally and can lull workers into a false sense of security. For example, Alan, a fifteen-year-old boy who had brutally knifed a girl of twelve, perplexed staff because he seemed to be pleasant and co-operative. The staff could not equate the details of his crime with the pleasant boy with whom they worked. The boy's counsellor, a young woman, made great efforts to get to know him and became alarmed when he started to make sexually suggestive remarks to her. She began to think of him as 'weird' and very frightening. His counselling was taken over by a consultant psychiatrist to whom the boy was able to confide that he had been having sexual fantasies about his counsellor. It soon became clear that this was a boy who found sexual feelings and fantasies utterly overwhelming. Indeed, when talking about the murder of the twelve-year-old girl he became very confused and said that he was frightened because he felt that she had been about to attack him. The psychiatrist came to the conclusion that the boy had felt attacked by his own sexual feelings about the girl, had projected these feelings onto the girl, and had then attacked them in her. Whilst he was in the grip of these feelings the boy was in effect in a psychotic and totally confused state in which the boundary between reality and fantasy had totally broken down. For much of the time, however, he was able to function normally.

(3) The histrionic adolescent

Many adolescents present their problems in a histrionic fashion. As indicated in the chapter on the nature of adolescence

(Chapter 1), this histrionic behaviour can commonly be misinterpreted as evidence of a developing schizophrenia. In practice, however, schizophrenia in adolescence usually presents as a profound perplexity or difficulty in thinking straight. For example, a sixteen-year-old girl, who was later diagnosed as having schizophrenia and who killed herself, originally presented with bursting into tears for no apparent reason. She had great difficulty in talking about what she thought was happening to her and had to write down her thoughts on a cigarette packet. A fifteen-year-old schizophrenic boy appeared to be quite normal until one day in the middle of writing an essay about the geography of Russia, he suddenly conceived the notion that he had a duty to reconvert Russia to Christianity. He tried to defend his views to his geography master and did not appear to be at all aware of the inconsistencies in his thinking. Only when so-called 'thought disorder' is present should a diagnosis of schizophrenia be made. Of course, when in doubt the opinion of a consultant psychiatrist should be sought.

Adolescents, in particular girls, can frequently cause alarm by presenting very strange ideas. For example, a fourteen-year-old girl maintained that she kept seeing on the wall the shadow of a woman with a knife in her hand. The girl was also getting into considerable trouble of a delinquent sort and was a source of great anxiety to her parents. The girl's symptoms rapidly abated, however, when one of the family 'secrets' was brought into the open. Like most such family secrets, everybody in the family knew about it but had felt unable to discuss it. The secret concerned the father's affair with one of his daughter's teachers. As another example of a bizarre and alarming idea, a seventeen-year-old girl complained to her counsellor that she kept imagining that there were men in her bed. She had names for all of these men and could feel them lying beside her. This seemed to be a similar experience to the imaginary companions that many younger children possess. The counsellor feared that the girl was going mad, but in fact the girl exhibited nothing in the way of thought disorder and indeed to some extent seemed to enjoy talking about her imaginary companions in order to intrigue her counsellor. It is important to remember that many disturbed adolescents will, if given the chance, play to the gallery. If they perceive that their counsellor is frightened, horrified, or excited by what they are presenting, they are quite capable of producing more exciting material in order to keep the attention of their counsellor and to avoid looking at issues that really trouble them. So-called suicidal attempts come into this category. Obviously any incidence of self-injury has to be taken seriously but it is unwise, especially in histrionic young girls, to make too much of it. There is a danger that everybody concerned can become so caught up in the drama of the suicidal attempt that day-to-day issues, such as how the young person is coping with relationships in the unit, are overlooked.

(4) The entrapping adolescent

Psychotherapy with a client of any age is a difficult exercise because its aim is to help the client to look at issues that are painful, not looked at in the light of day, and have the power to affect the client's behaviour. In ways that are largely unconscious, the client will constantly seek to thwart the efforts of the therapist. Adolescents can be particularly adept at this. Psychotherapy with adolescents can resemble a game of chess in which the adolescent seeks to entrap and to checkmate the therapist. The following are some of the more common methods of entrapment:

(1) Occasionally adolescents will say that they think it unfair that they have to talk about their problems while the therapist remains silent about their own. Whilst adult patients can complain of the same unfairness as they see it, most of them do also recognize that if they are to get help they have to talk about their problems rather than listening to the therapist's. Adolescents, however, have a tendency to see this as grossly unfair and can be very persistent on this issue. On occasion, therapists can get trapped into volunteering to talk about their own problems in order to help the adolescent talk more freely. Although they may invite it, this is, as a rule, very alarming for the adolescent concerned. This is not to say that therapists should not talk about their own experience of life and its difficulties, but such a

discussion should take place when and where the therapist, not the adolescent, feels it to be appropriate.

(2) The adolescent may ask whether the therapist really cares for him or her. This usually goes along with a statement such as 'You are only doing this because you get paid to' or 'You don't really care'. It is a mistake to try to convince the adolescent that one 'really does care'. After all, 'really caring' in this context means that the therapist has a duty to point out the ways in which the adolescent is trying to control the therapist by the use of such manoeuvres.

(3) A particularly difficult form of entrapment for residential social workers to cope with in individual counselling comes from the adolescent who says that there are some things they can tell only to their counsellor and which must not be repeated to other members of the staff. Frequently this will be a confession of some sort of delinquent act and if the staff member becomes bound to silence, he or she can, in effect, seem to be condoning delinquency by keeping quiet about it. There is no easy answer to this dilemma because obviously one of the points of having an individual counsellor is to be able to speak with him or her more freely than in a group. In our experience, however, it is usually best, if the adolescent is trying to swear you to silence, to make the point that in your experience this is largely unhelpful and if they cannot share the secret with the other young people and staff it would be best not to talk about it for the time being.

CONCLUSION

The roles of caregiver, custodian, and counsellor are difficult to combine. In our experience no institution is able to combine them perfectly. However, residential social workers, like ordinary parents, do not have to be perfect they just have to be, to use Winnicott's phrase, 'good enough'.

3 The Worker in Groups

In this chapter we shall be discussing the role of the residential social worker in different types of group – family group, adolescent group, and staff support group.

(1) FAMILY GROUPS

In recent years there has been a great deal of interest in trying to understand young people's problems within the setting of their families. Although most of this work has been carried out in the out-patient departments of child psychiatric clinics and in child guidance units, it is now being extended to work with adolescents in residential settings.

Most family therapists base their work upon what is generally described as a systems approach. This is a fundamentally different way of looking at people's problems. Instead of regarding such problems as a quality of the individual, problems are thought of as an attempt expressed through an individual to stabilize the social system within which he or she is living. Usually this social system is the family. For example, a thirteen-year-old boy presented with problems of stealing and over-eating. An individual therapist might have tried to understand his problems in terms of a chemical imbalance in his brain, or of a personality disorder determined partly by his genetic endowment and partly by his past experience. In practice the problem was dealt with by a family therapist who thought of the boy's problems as being an attempt to stabilize the family system by drawing attention away from the parents' very considerable marital problems. The parents were able to avoid looking at their problems because their emotional energy was diverted into worrying about their son's difficulties. However, once the parents were able to face their problems of living together, the boy was able to cease his unconscious attempt to stabilize the family system and his symptoms abated. In this family system this happened relatively easily but in some families, of course, the problems underlying the symptoms are so great that the family therapist's attempt to move the family away from maladaptive modes of functioning are severely resisted.

In our experience the greatest difficulty encountered by the residential social worker trying to do family therapy is the shift away from viewing an adolescent's difficulties as being the result of what parents have done (that is, seeing the adolescent as a victim), to seeing the family system as a whole in which everybody is a victim of maladaptive ways of coping. The difficulty in this shift of emphasis is compounded by the fact that in many ways residential social workers are expected to function as substitute parents. The implication of this is that in a profound way the child's previous parenting has been lacking and that the residential social worker has to make up for what has been missed. Inevitably this places the residential social worker in the position of a rival to the adolescent's natural parents. This situation can be easily exploited by adolescents in order to play off their residential social workers against their own parents. In many ways this is a situation similar to that experienced by the children of estranged parents. Very commonly such children come to regard one parent as the 'out-parent' (the bad parent who has brought about the split-up in the marriage), and the other parent as the 'in-parent' (the good parent who is the victim of his or her spouse). Residential social workers may find themselves put in the position of being 'in-parent' or 'out-parent' in relation to the natural parent. Either situation is equally unhelpful to the adolescent because the idealization of one parent or substitute parent at the expense of the other enables the adolescent to retreat into a way of thinking about the world in which someone somewhere is going to come along and magically help with his or her difficulties. Only by being helped to see people as they really are – that is, a mixture of good and bad qualities – is the adolescent to receive the best from people who are available to help. If the adolescent is constantly in a position of feeling that others do not match up to some ideal, then the feeling of being hard done by and of being justified in exploiting people, if necessary in a delinquent way, continues.

At this point it would be useful to give a couple of examples of adolescents who tried to split residential staff from their own parents. Peter, aged fourteen, had been admitted to a closed institution because of arson offences. He had burnt down his school with what appeared to be a totally ruthless disregard for other people's safety. Peter had been adopted at the age of two and before his adoption had a very unsettled and upsetting existence. He had been cared for in a number of institutions and had also been in hospital on a number of occasions for a bowel disorder. He had always appeared cold and indifferent to his adoptive parents. For example, on one occasion, at Christmas time, they had put his presents outside his door and had waited in excited anticipation of his response. Peter stepped over the presents without a second glance and appeared totally uninterested in what his adoptive parents had given him. For the duration of his first year in the institution he presented considerable problems of management but gradually settled and became very attached to the particular residential social worker responsible for him. However, his attitude to his adoptive parents, having previously been one of apparent indifference, became one of hatred. On one occasion, having absconded from the institution with a number of his friends, he broke into his parent's house, stole some money, did a certain amount of damage, and defecated on the sitting-room carpet. His parents were in despair about him and thought of cutting off contact with him altogether. The residential social worker thought Peter's mother was uncaring and hard. The parents, in their turn, felt that the social worker was deliberately taking their son away from them and that if anything his behaviour was getting worse. After a series of family meetings, which were organized by an outside therapist and which included Peter, his social worker, and his parents, Peter's mother was able to begin to talk about her despair and her sense of guilt. After this, Peter's behaviour began to settle. He was able to go home for weekends and eventually, after leaving the institution, returned home permanently and eventually did well for himself.

Jane, aged fifteen, provides an example of an adolescent who idealized her parents at the expense of the residential social workers looking after her. Jane had been admitted to a closed institution because of kidnapping two small babies. She looked after the babies well and they were soon returned to their mothers. The kidnappings occurred a few months after Jane had been out shopping with her younger sister and this sister had been killed in a traffic accident. The family had always been very disorganized and had suffered a good deal of marital disharmony. Both parents were themselves very deprived as children and had difficulty in being adequate parents to their own children. Following the death of his daughter, the father became very withdrawn.

After she had been admitted to the closed institution, Jane wrote a number of letters to her parents in which she expressed guilt about her younger sister's death (though there was no evidence whatsoever that she had in fact contributed to it). It was clear that Jane had kidnapped the two babies in order to try to make up for the lost child in her own family. For a considerable time she was unable to settle in the institution and was resentful and suspicious of the residential social worker looking after her. She tended to play off the residential staff against her parents, and the latter made frequent complaints about how their daughter was being dealt with. In their turn, the residential staff felt that the parents were obstructive, delinquent, and cunning. Eventually, in order to try to calm the situation, a series of family sessions run by an outside consultant was set up. As in Peter's case, this included Jane, her residential social worker, her parents, and her remaining brothers and sisters. Many issues were talked about in these meetings but the turning point came when the whole family was able to relive the death of Jane's younger sister. For the first time Jane's father in particular was able to face his grief and in acknowledging it to lift the burden of guilt that Jane had had to bear. He was able to talk about his own feeling that he had let his dead daughter down and that he frequently felt guilty and incompetent as a father and husband.

He did not much change his ways as a result of this acknowledge-ment, but Jane was better able to make use of the good experi-ences the institution was able to provide her with and eventually she was able to return home. In a subsequent letter to her resi-dential social worker she wrote 'My parents are awful but they will do and I love them'.

In both of the above examples the residential social workers did not themselves act as the family therapists. It is extremely difficult, if not impossible, to be simultaneously a substitute parent and somebody who is able to look dispassionately at the child's family system. It is usually better for the family therapy to be conducted by an outside therapist and for the residential social worker to be included as a part of the family system. Some residential social workers find this difficult because it means that their own motives and behaviour have to be examined along with those of the natural parents. In our experience, however, if they are prepared to do this they are richly rewarded by a better relationship with the child and the parents. If the natural parents can see the residential social worker struggling as much as they are, they feel less envious and are less destructive of the child's relationship with the social worker.

There are a number of ways in which residential social workers can prepare themselves for family therapy and make themselves more aware of the child's family of origin. The simplest method is, of course, to make the effort to meet with the child's parents and to discuss the child's family background. Some residential social workers (and indeed it is the policy of some institutions) leave discussions with the child's parents to outside social workers. In our experience, however, if a residen-tial social worker continues with this system they are depriving themselves of vital information about the child in their care and are more easily prey to adopting critical attitudes to the child's parents. For example, a middle-aged residential social worker became very attached to one of the children in her charge. This was a sixteen-year-old boy who had come to the institution because of a number of episodes in which he had behaved in a very dangerous fashion; in particular he had threatened two women on two separate occasions with a knife. He had spent many years in institutions and had been more or less dumped on the doorstep of a children's home by his mother when he was seven years old. The mother made little attempt to visit him in the institution and the boy's residential social worker felt critical of her. Her attitude modified, however, when the mother was encouraged to visit and to stay in the institution and was able to talk about her own life. She had always been a very violent woman and had on one occasion cut off a piece of her husband's ear. When she had been a girl she had contracted tuberculosis and had been admitted to hospital where she lived for many years. During her time there her own mother and father hardly ever visited her and when she returned home in her early teens it was to virtual strangers. Needless to say, merely having discussions about her previous life did not alter her cruel attitude to her children but it enabled the residential staff to feel less critical towards her and to communicate this altered attitude to the boy.

Residential social workers' attitudes to the parents of adolescents are, of course, in part determined by the worker's own experience in their family of origin. If they have had particular family difficulties themselves they may find these especially painful to have to face in the families of the children they are looking after. It can be extremely useful for the worker to be helped to see how their own family experiences affect their work. There are a number of ways in which workers can sharpen up their family therapy skills and these are well described in a number of text books such as that by Robin Skynner (1976). One example to illustrate the sort of techniques that can be used is a worker who describes how confused and lost she felt when she met the parents of a child in her care. She was invited to take part in a role-play of the family session. Some of her fellow residential social workers took the part of the family and she tried to discuss some of the family problems with them. She briefed her fellow workers about the characters and difficulties of the family members they were to portray. She was then asked to conduct a family session as she would normally do. She was, however, asked to signal when she started to feel confused. After about ten minutes she indicated that she was getting lost and at this point was asked to set up another role-play depicting a scene from her own family of origin when she was a little girl. The scene started at the family breakfast table but this brought back memories of her parents' rows which she felt unable to bear when she was a child. Her reaction had been to hide behind the curtains in order to get away from them. It became clear that she became lost and confused in her family work whenever parents were beginning to talk about their difficulties together and when there was a danger that they might start to explode into furious rowing.

In addition to in-service training in family therapy, there are now many courses (for example, those run by the Institute of Family Therapy in London) available for residential social workers to improve their family therapy skills. If a few keen workers from an institution are able to attend such courses they are usually able to carry their experience back to their colleagues.

(2) GROUP THERAPY WITH ADOLESCENTS

There are four main types of group work with adolescents. The first type involves an informal group. Such groups tend to form from time to time in all but the most rigidly controlled adolescent units. These are the discussion groups that occur at meal times, or around the television set, or in the evening when young people tend to drift into the staff office. They are an important aspect of institutional life with adolescents who usually value these occasions because of their informality and because it is under their control whether they take part in them or not.

The second type of group is the so-called community meeting. These have been mentioned before (Chapter 2) when we talked about the therapeutic community approach that many adolescent units adopt. Community meetings attended by all the young people and the staff on duty should, in our opinion, be an integral part of even the most formal of adolescent units. They are one way of using day-to-day events to help young people function more effectively. They give young people practice in putting their experiences into words and they also help to head off what Balbernie (1972) has called the 'life between the floor-boards', which tends to occur in even the best regulated of insti-tutions. By this Balbernie means, of course, all of the informal communications and activities, often deliquent, that are never examined openly. For example, on a couple of occasions a young and extremely inexperienced residential social worker had lent some money to one of the adolescent boys in his unit. He had not thought to mention this to other staff members. One morning in a community meeting one of the young people said that the boy had been boasting about being able to get money out of the staff. This led to a useful discussion of the way in which staff could be conned and to a certain amount of joking (and yet at the same time very serious) remarks about whether the money had been for homosexual services. It also became apparent that the young people watched each other very closely for what they were getting from the staff in terms of attention and in the meeting they were able to begin to look at their tremendous jealousy of each other. In a subsequent staff sup-port meeting the young staff member was able to see how he had used giving money to bolster his own sense of inadequacy and to see how, in fact, he had been rather frightened of the boy and in a sense had bought him off.

The third type of group encountered in adolescent units is the so-called experiential group. They are called experiential because the emphasis is on activity designed to give expression to emotions rather than on discussions of thoughts and feelings. Dunne *et al.* (1982) have given an excellent description of this type of group and use them extensively in their work at the ado-lescent unit at Hill End Hospital in Hertfordshire. Experiential groups take as their starting point the notion that powerful thoughts and emotions can be locked up in posture, gesture, and muscular tension. Only through bodily action can the memories be unlocked and come into consciousness where they can be examined. As an example, Bruggen (1979) cites the case of a fifteen-year-old girl who had been brought up by her aunt dur-ing the many admissions of her mother to a psychiatric hospital. In Bruggen's unit the parents are involved in experiential groups and on the occasion in question the girl was being rocked by both her mother and aunt.

'The group of staff and family in the session was arranged so that each maternal figure was on either side of the girl's trunk and shoulders. As they rocked her, the position of the maternal arms changed from being underneath the girl to being, in each case, one underneath and one on top, as if each mother was preparing to pull the girl away from the other. The girl sat up in terror. The tug of love had been visibly reproduced for both of them and the girl to see and re-examine. The interpretation could then be made that behind her continuing rebuff of any adult care, lay an anxiety of its leading to such a terrible being torn in two feeling.'

(Bruggen 1979 : 227)

In our experience of setting up experiential groups in units for adolescents the staff have to prepare themselves very carefully before embarking upon experiential work with the adolescents themselves. The staff should go through the exercises in the staff group and so be forewarned of their powerfulness. Some staff members find such exercises extremely difficult to take part in and on occasions they may try to belittle them. In our experience, unless all the staff members are prepared to commit themselves to such work, a serious division can occur in the unit and the programme of experiential exercises does not firmly take root.

The fourth type of group encountered in adolescent units is the small psychotherapy group. Much has been written about such groups and the reader is referred to the work of Acton (1970), Bruce (1975), and Steinberg *et al.* (1978) who look particularly at group work with adolescents. For a general overview of group-work practice, the reader is referred to the writings of Tom Douglas (1976, 1978, and 1983).

Small group psychotherapy is not simply individual psychotherapy with a number of people. The group therapist not only looks at the way in which individuals are discussing their problems in a group, but also tries to tune into what the group as a whole is doing. Groups, like individuals, put up resistances to looking at problems. For example, the whole group may adopt a passive stance in relation to the group therapist and try to manœuvre the therapist into a question-and-answer session rather than trying to work out for themselves how they want the group to run. Other forms of group resistance to change are, to use the terminology of one of the pioneer group therapists, Wilfred Bion (1959), 'pairing' and 'fight and flight'. In the pairing manoeuvre individual group members get together in pairs and so exclude themselves from what is happening in the rest of the group. In the fight and flight manoeuvre the group members either bicker about what they should be discussing in the group or opt to talk about some neutral and unthreatening topic such as the latest films they have seen.

Adolescent groups are particularly characterized by their tendency to turn into fight and flight groups. Adolescents may quite literally get so angry with each other that the group therapist has to stop a fight developing, and many adolescents have very great difficulty in staying in the room throughout the group session. For example, Joan, a fifteen-year-old girl, had had in the first three years of her life a number of hospital admissions with dislocated hips and severe vomiting which necessitated an operation on her stomach. She almost certainly also had a minor degree of brain damage. She presented at the age of fourteen, after her parents' marriage had broken up, in a wildly delinquent state. She would stay out late or indeed all night. She was sexually promiscuous and had experimented with a large number of different types of drugs. When she was admitted to the adolescent unit she was so self-destructive that her life was feared for. She tended to vilify the workers looking after her. In group therapy she tended to be contemptuous of the efforts of the therapist to look at what was happening in the group, but this was clearly a cover for severe anxiety. She found it literally impossible to sit in a group for longer than about fifteen minutes. If she did not actually leave the room she would pace up and down like an animal in a cage. If she was put next to the group therapist she managed to stay for a little longer but usually she had left the group before it had finished. Because of this tendency for adolescent groups to resort to fight and flight, therapists are involved to a greater extent than therapists of adult groups in limit-setting and direct confrontation.

The three main sources of difficulty for adolescent group therapists are social, cognitive, and emotional. These difficulties are consequences of the adolescent process, the details of which have been described in Chapter 1 on the nature of adolescence.

(1) Social difficulty

In discussing the work of Erik Erikson (1968) (pp. 10–11), attention has already been drawn to the tendency for adolescents to get together in groups or gangs. Gang formation is particularly evident in large cities. In a city such as Edinburgh, for example, there are gang slogans scrawled on the walls of bus shelters. Each gang seems to have its own territory and they have names such as Barox, Niddrie Terrors, Suicide Squad, Gorgie Jungle, Young Leith Team, Young Mental Drylaw, and Tollcross Rebels. These names tend to conjure up vivid pictures that are in strong contrast to the picture presented by individual members of the gang when one meets them on their own. The boys and girls who run with these gangs often have very impoverished emotional and intellectual lives. It is as though the gang gives them a corporate identity which they lack individually. According to Erikson's theory, this can be thought of in terms of the difficulties that many young people have in acquiring adult identities for themselves. As they withdraw from their parents they are in need of the gang to act as a stake on which to tie their developing identities. This process can present difficulties for a group therapist. One of the points about being in an adolescent group or gang is that there are no adults around. It is because an adolescent wishes to keep grown-ups out that they seek a gang. It is therefore very usual for therapists working with adolescent groups to feel that they are being kept at bay or are excluded. Certainly it is very common for therapists in an adolescent group to feel that they have nothing at all to offer these young people.

(2) Cognitive difficulty

David Elkind's (1967) work has already been touched upon in Chapter 1. With the onset of adolescence, young people begin to think in terms of abstract concepts. However, it should always be remembered that their ability to do so is still very immature. They still have great difficulty in standing back from their own mental processes and observing what they are doing. Group therapists may therefore find that they have gone beyond the ability of the group to understand what is going on if they try to work in a very abstract way. For example, if the therapist points out that the various ways in which the young people are behaving in the group are manouevres designed to avoid anxiety, the young people may simply not understand what is meant. Young people also have great difficulty in appreciating that other people's experiences are relevant to their own. This can sometimes be mistaken for selfishness, but in our opinion it is much more frequently the result of the young persons' immaturity with regard to abstract thinking. A group therapist working with young people has therefore in some ways to function like the leader of a toddlers' group. If the therapist is to hold the attention of some of the members of the group, he or she has to say something about what each of them is doing rather than using a general statement covering the whole group. It is also wise for the group therapist to be very direct. For example, when a boy was ostentatiously reading whilst the group therapist was talking, the therapist stopped and said 'When you read your book, Graham, it makes me feel that I have been talking nonsense. Could you please put it away?'. It is always best for group therapists to say how they are being affected by what the group members are doing rather than to try to impose discipline in an authoritarian fashion.

(3) Emotional difficulty

Reference has already been made to Donald Winnicot's view of adolescence (see pp. 12–14). As a rule, adolescents who are in need of group therapy have had early experiences in which they have not felt safe to make normal childhood demands upon parents whom they could trust fully. Disturbed adolescents in groups therefore have a tendency to gang together to test out the group therapist. They will often push therapists to the limits of their patience and ability to cope in order to make quite sure that they can survive such attacks. On occasion these attacks are verbal but they can also be physical. As an example of verbal attacks we quote from the notes of a therapist who was standing in for the usual group therapist who was away ill. One of the boys started off by saying to the stand-in therapist 'Who are you anyway?'. (The boy knew perfectly well.) One of the girls, Frances, said 'Oh, he's a nutter'. Then another boy said, 'When Stephen [the usual group therapist] is here we all huddle round the fire. Today we are all spaced out and cold. It's horrible.' Then Frances looked at the stand-in therapist's black sweater and said, 'He's in the SS'. It was difficult for the stand-in therapist to convey the strength of the feelings being directed at him. He felt like giving up and walking out. However, he stayed and although throughout the session the young people, furious that they had been abandoned by the usual therapist, needed to attack his substitute again and again, the group was also able to think a little about the agonies of separation and loss.

It should be obvious from the above descriptions that group work with adolescents can be a most exacting experience for the person undertaking it. Anybody embarking upon such work should have available a supervision group in which they can share experiences in the group with other group therapists and get guidance from a supervision group leader. Because of the great need that adolescents have for consistency, no-one should embark on group work with adolescents unless they can give a minimum of six months to the project.

(3) STAFF SUPPORT GROUPS

At this point it will be appropriate to discuss the sort of issues and difficulties that arise in staff support groups. Such groups may be set up to supervise a particular activity such as group therapy by its members, or it may simply be a group in which anything of relevance to the work of the adolescent unit can be discussed. In our experience, staff support groups that meet less frequently than once a week have great difficulty in achieving a sense of cohesion and continuity. Staff support meetings should be held at a regular time each week and like all groups there should be clearly defined time boundaries. Frequently staff will only feel safe to bring up painful issues within the last quarter of an hour of the meeting and they are denied this haven of safety if the meeting is on a flexi-time basis. Support groups are usually best run by an outside consultant who is able to view the processes of the institution dispassionately and disinterestedly. Where possible, all members of staff on a particular unit should attend the staff support meeting. To try to run staff support groups with individual shifts deepens divisions within a unit and leads to a lack of cohesion in overall policy. The person directly responsible for the unit should attend but, in our experience, staff support groups should not be attended by a member of management staff who has responsibility for a number of units within an institution. If possible, he or she should attend a staff support group together with the heads of units. In our experience the attendance of the Head of an institution has an inhibiting effect on the meeting and the Head does not feel able to participate fully in front of the most junior members of staff.

In our experience there is usually a certain amount of resistance to the setting up of staff support groups. Whilst there is usually a core of staff members who want to have such groups, there is usually another group that feels that staff support groups are an implicit criticism of the way they are working and that they, and their methods of working, are going to be examined and criticized. In our experience, however, it is not necessarily the most enthusiastic initial supporters of the group idea who turn out to be the most effective members. Quite frequently, staff members who express a certain amount of scepticism contribute a good deal to the work of the group, whilst initially very enthusiastic members end up by being disappointed that the inauguration of the staff support group does not lead to a transformation in the conditions and quality of their work.

Before any system of staff support meetings can get off the ground, the absolute co-operation of the Head of the institution has to be sought and gained. If this support is not forthcoming, the group leader will find all sorts of obstacles put in the way of the group. Examples that we have encountered include 'The usual room used by the group being used for a meeting of the management committee'; 'Because of shortage of staff the group will have to be cancelled today'; 'Because it is such a lovely day we decided to send the kids out for a picnic and so there is nobody left in the building'. Even with the co-operation of the Head, resistance is to be expected from individual staff members. Staff may turn up late or not at all, frequently with impeccable excuses. If the group leader does not at least make an attempt to call attention to such absences, the person doing the absconding may paradoxically feel rather let down and think their absence has been of such little importance that it has gone unnoticed. Staff support groups are technically difficult because whilst the group leader may know the group members quite intimately through other aspects of the unit's work, he or she may feel inhibited about drawing attention to what is going on in the group in a way that the leader of an out-patient psycho-therapy group would not.

In our experience, staff support groups have a tendency to go through a series of crises with lulls inbetween. If a group is being effective it is always to some extent painful and difficult. On the other hand, it should not be so exhausting that the group leader and the members feel unable to carry on. In the early days of a group the crises usually centre on confusion about the problems to be discussed. The group tends to oscillate (expression is often given to these oscillations by particular members of the group) between whether intensely personal issues should be discussed or whether the group should stick safely to set topics. Frequently the subjects of these set topics indicate the group's underlying fears about itself. For example, one group thought that it might like to discuss how to deal with particularly deprived adolescents. After some discussion of this issue it became clear to the group leader that the members were really talking about how many of their own needs the group members felt able to bring into the group for discussion. If the group leader can identify an underlying anxiety of this sort, then this usually leads to a sense of relief in the group. The group can then move on to a different and more personal plane of discussion. The early days of the group are also often characterized by long silences and there is usually one member who will use these silences to illustrate the point that such groups are a waste of time. It is important for the group leader not to get into a position where he or she is justifying the value of the group in spite of the silences. Where possible, the leader should help the group to discuss the uselessness or value of the silence for themselves. Indeed, in general, as with psychotherapy groups, the group leader should avoid getting into a position where he or she is turned to as a sort of oracle that will answer all of the groups problems. The leader need not maintain an implacable silence when asked a direct question about a particular problem; an opinion can be given and the group can be asked to discuss the issue in question.

In almost every staff support group there are three levels of discussion: (1) Discussion about relationships between staff; (2) Discussion about individual adolescents; (3) Some indication of the staff's home or social life.

(1) Discussion about staff working relationships

One of the main reasons for having staff support groups is so that staff may support each other in their work. To take an example, a residential social worker became extremely distressed following the death from cancer of one of the adolescents in her care. The onset of the disease had been sudden and its course rapid and unstoppable. Although the residential social worker knew at an intellectual level that there was nothing she could have done to avert the course of the disease, she could not help reproaching herself. This issue was discussed during a number of staff support meetings and, in addition to the general comforting she received from her fellow workers, she was also able to look at why she had been so profoundly hurt. She was the oldest of eight children. It seemed to her when she was a girl that her mother was constantly pregnant and preoccupied. It had largely fallen on her to look after the older children and she had had to become 'a little mother' before she had the emotional resources to cope with the demands of this task. The death of the child in her care overwhelmed her poorly established defences which had been erected to function as if she really were a well-integrated grown-up able to cope with life's vicissitudes. In fact, behind these defences she felt like a frightened and overwhelmed child and it was this side of her that came to the fore under severe stress. Subsequent to this crisis this particular worker was able to be less of a coper on her own and was better able to turn to others for help when she felt overwhelmed. Hers was an example of a life crisis that was used to further personality development rather than to stunt it.

Another example of the latter, although of a less dramatic kind, is provided by a residential social worker in his late twenties who had gone into work with disturbed adolescents because he felt that they were given a 'raw deal' by society. In the staff support meetings he tended to be extremely critical of the leader of his unit and of the consultant who was running the staff support group. Although he was a good and conscientious worker, at times he could be extremely irritating, taking issue over almost every decision that had to be made. Many of his criticisms were justified and the work of the unit was modified as a result. This process has been described by David Clark (1974) as 'harnessing the indignation of the young'. Gradually, however, largely through the comments of the workers of his own age or younger, he came to see that he was looking for a fight for a fight's sake. He was able to relate his present attitudes to his fear of, and anger towards, his army officer father who had been something of a family martinet. As an adolescent he had suffered a terrible blow when his sister was killed in an accident. He had felt responsible for this and his dedication to young people was in part an attempt to expiate his own guilt. At one point in his attempt to understand himself in the staff support groups he became quite despairing of his ability to contribute anything to the institution. However, he managed to get through this crisis and to see that although the young people in his care would only make limited gains, they would not make any progress at all, or would even get worse, if they were not helped by people in his position. He was able to begin to take a gentler view of authority, decided to stay on at the institution, and eventually became the successful leader of one of the units in the institution.

Apart from support over deeply personal issues, staff support groups provide a forum in which personality clashes amongst staff members may be examined and discussed. A healthy institution needs, and should encourage, people of different personality types to work together. The ability to face and contain inevitable clashes of personality is an index of the health of the institution. For example, a unit had been going through a difficult time with a lot of delinquent behaviour on the part of the young people. The cause of this tension was initially not obvious. It was clear, however, that the staff were unable to work in a co-ordinated fashion towards helping the young people. Eventually a spokesman for a particular shift said that he simply could not stomach the authoritarian attitude of the leader of the unit. He felt that the leader was being dictatorial and that he was not allowing enough individual initiative. The house leader in his turn felt that as the unit was going through a crisis he needed to be very firm and definite in the decisions he made about how the unit should be run. Eventually many of staff members were able to talk about the difficulties imposed by the house leader's engagement to one of the members of staff of the unit. The staff felt that because of the special relationship between the leader and his fiancée there were in fact two leaders of the unit. They felt that whatever they did when the leader was absent was reported back to him by his fiancée. These were difficult matters to discuss and to some extent were unresolvable. However, the fact that the staff were able to bring such painful issues out into the open helped the unit to survive a difficult period in its history.

A general point may be made here about the difficulties imposed by the shift system operating in most adolescent units. Sophia Benson *et al.* (1976), writing about the work of the Hill

End adolescent unit have described the phenomenon of 'cliquism', which tends to arise when staff work for an appreciable length of time on the same shift. Inevitably, each shift tends to develop its own ways of working and disturbed young people are very quick to point out and exploit the differences in practice between shifts. Hand-over meetings from one shift to another only go part of the way to resolving this problem. If a unit is going through a tough time, the shifts can coalesce for sometime into rigid cliques which view the work of other shifts askance. For this reason, as indicated earlier in this chapter (p. 50) the members of all shifts should attend staff support meetings. Also, from time to time members of shifts should be moved around although there are frequently complaints from staff about this.

(2) Discussion about the adolescents

Staff support groups are a useful supplement to case conferences and reviews of adolescents because they can allow a freer discussion of adolescent problems and their effects on the staff. Case conferences are frequently attended by outside social workers and staff may not feel entirely free to discuss in front of them how a particular adolescent is affecting them. In the staff support group differences of opinion about policy can be brought into the open and post mortems can be conducted where things have gone wrong. Frequently things go wrong because of failure in communication between staff members. Every adolescent unit will have its own collection of such events. For example, a fourteen-year-old girl in a semi-secure unit was being visited by her father whom she had not met for a number of years. Staff members on the early shift had some doubts about the father and had made it clear that they wanted the visit to be confined to the unit. However, they failed to communicate this to the next shift who allowed the girl to go out with her father 'for a walk'. The father helped his daughter to abscond and she was away from the unit for a number of days.

Staff support groups are also an appropriate place for staff to talk about their feelings towards the adolescents. It should be recognized that staff not only have angry or loving feelings towards adolescents, they may also on occasion feel sexually attracted towards them. This is a topic that is very rarely discussed or written about but staff can gain considerable relief and freedom from unneccesary guilt if they are able to share with each other their feelings of sexual attraction towards particular boys or girls. The staff support group should also be the place where the attraction of this sort can be talked about before it gets out of hand.

On occasion, of course, differences of opinion about how a particular adolescent should be managed may be a cover for underlying staff difficulties. In a unit in which there were both teachers and residential social workers, the social workers felt that more emphasis should be put upon a particular adolescent's education. After some initial discussion about the advantages and disadvantages of this change of emphasis, it became clear that in fact the residential social workers were saying that they felt unsupported by the teachers. The residential social workers felt that whenever there was a crisis in the classroom they were called in to sort it out. They felt that the teachers were not taking their fair share of the hard knocks whilst claiming to have more of a say in how the unit should be run. If such differences are not fully discussed, the particular adolescent can become a pawn and, as a result, can become very disturbed. Goffmann (1968) and Stanton and Schwartz (1954) have discussed a similar phenomenon in psychiatric hospitals where patients can present with an exacerbation of their psychiatric illness when staff battles are being fought over them.

(3) Home and social difficulties of staff

Most staff support groups have an explicit or implicit understanding that home or social matters should only be discussed where they affect the work of the unit. In practice, however, the demands of working with disturbed adolescents are such that even the smallest personal upset can have an affect on a person's functioning. For example, a female residential social worker who was pregnant started to become very irritable with young people. The staff in her unit knew this was in part because of the physical effects of her pregnancy but also because she felt unsupported by her husband. In the end they felt that her work was being so badly affected that the issue had to be brought to a staff support group. In this instance the woman felt supported by having her problems recognized openly. On other occasions, however, it is much more appropriate for problems to be dealt with outside the group and staff should have an outside counsellor available to them when needed.

It should be recognized that staff derive support from many different sources. They may receive it from their home, or from the social life they lead with other staff members. Of course, they also derive support directly from their work with young people when this is going well. It tends to be staff members higher up the management hierachy, and who are at a greater distance from the young people, who are most reliant on staff support groups.

CONCLUSION

Almost any activity that staff engage in with disturbed adolescents can at times be emotionally exhausting. We have emphasized the importance of staff support groups to sustain staff in their task, but, of course, some staff will wish to complement their skills by having personal therapy, either in a group or individually, in order to alert them to areas of conflict within their personalities which they bring to their work. At present, however, group and individual psychotherapy is, unfortunately, not readily available outside the largest centres in the United Kingdom.

4 The Need for Team-Work Skills

In most residential establishments the wide range of caring tasks and therapeutic interventions that together comprise the residential task are most often carried out by teams of staff instead of individuals. Much of the literature on training residential staff refers to skills necessary to effect change in the young person on the basis of some intervention or personal contact. As we have seen, included in this category are counselling skills, supervision skills, and personal relationships, plus all the 'back-up' knowledge that accompanies these skills. We refer to this group of skills as contact skills.

However, the quality of residential care is not solely determined by the presence, in effective quantities, of these contact skills. The very way in which a residential team works together to pool their resources in order to provide the best possible care and treatment is in itself an important influencing factor in determining the quality of residential care. Characteristics of the staff world are important in determining the overall effectiveness of the organization (Jacques 1955; Menzies 1970; Harris and Anderson 1979; Millham *et al.* 1980) and the capacity to work harmoniously and effectively with one's colleagues have long been recognized as essential requirements for residential work. One of the main causes of high turnover in residential establishments has been found to be staff inability to resolve interpersonal conflicts and disputes, including those with senior staff.

Some writers (Yalom 1958 and Douglas 1978, for example) recognize the need for specific skills to be taught as prerequisites of effective group membership. Groups can be seen as vehicles for learning a wide range of effective social and interpersonal skills (Yalom 1958). Harris and Anderson (1979) note that much real-life training for social work and residential work occurs in the on-site situation, and that learning is mediated by both informal instruction from colleagues and by observing the behaviour of more experienced workers. Douglas (1976) has commented on the need to recognize the behaviour of groups that are effective in influencing members' behaviour, which in turn is often motivated by the desire to be recognized by, or included in, the group. As most new staff are presumably well motivated to become included in their new work group, and because they will possess a natural desire to be recognized for the personal and professional levels of expertise they are bringing to the group, the climate of the residential team, in both structural and psychological terms, needs to be constantly monitored by the members themselves as well as outside consultants so that the most beneficial learning atmosphere for residential staff can be developed. Krause (1974), in his study of attitudes amongst residential staff, found that the prevailing attitudes of the residential team, both towards explicit child-care issues and personal attitudinal standpoints concerning authoritarianism and dogmatism, were more potent factors in moulding and determining the eventual working characteristics of new staff than were their previous learning, training, and experience. This process of institutional socialization is reflected in the problems that Karl Menninger (1971) describes in the assimilation of new staff and their attitudes and expectations into the clinical team.

THE NATURE OF THE TEAM

Webb (in Stevenson 1977) has identified four models of teamwork practice. The first, the *collegial* team, describes a work group composed of equal status workers. A derivative of this model, the *specialized collegial* team, is composed of staff who specialize by virtue of tasks but where no hierarchy need be implied or seen. In the third team model, the *apprenticeship* team, the same task is shared by all team members, regardless of types or levels of possessed skills. Webb's fourth model, the *complex* team, is characterized by a climate in which both tasks and skills vary. Stevenson (1977) concluded that the fourth model inevitably will emerge in social work departments. In residential care, where an integrated staff team work together with the client group for a period of time, Webb's analysis is not so easy to apply in a general form as the characteristics of that team will vary according to the type of institution and its specific goals. In some establishments teams are characterized by specialization of function, e.g. teaching and child care. In these cases the 'smooth flow of work', as Webb describes it, will depend on the extent to which there is a conflict of roles and a misunderstanding of the nature of the formal or informal hierarchy within the team. Tension between professional groups within teams, based upon an assessment of the significance of their own specialized contributions, and reinforced, or contradicted, by structural factors such as conditions of service and salary (tensions noted by Millham *et al.* (1980) in their study of security units), has led to much reappraisal of staffing structure within establishments.

A more recent model of residential staff structure, known as group work, has developed, partly as a response to the need to remove some of the more debilitating tensions in classical residential teams, where specialization by virtue of task and professional background has been the norm. It is characterized by a sharing of responsibility for all aspects of residential care in a way that cuts across professional training boundaries. Thus, teachers can legitimately participate in non-educational activities, and non-teaching staff (i.e. child-care officers and nurses) can make a valuable and acknowledged contribution to educational programmes. In practice this model of team work, with its implications for the removal of professional hierarchies based on status and inter-professional tensions, requires considerable organizational support for it to become established and to function effectively. Lack of task specialization can lead to inconsistency in task implementation unless residential tasks and activities are constantly monitored and supported. New staff may feel threatened by removal of status satisfactions imposed by previous professional background, and feel also that they will have to participate in professional activities for which they do not feel qualified: for example, child-care staff may be concerned or anxious at the thought of teaching disturbed young people. Specialization by task, if dictated by an assessment of the needs of the client population, will be dictated by a match of needs to skills and resources, which may not parallel professional boundaries. In this sense, group-work practice approaches Webb's second model in which specialization by task does not involve a hierarchy. Specialized coordinated programmes of residential activities need to be staffed in such a way as to promote consistency, continuity, and an appropriate degree of structure and planning from which young people can derive maximum benefit.

TEAM-BASED TRAINING AS A BASIS FOR IN-SERVICE TRAINING

As Stevenson *et al.* (1977 : 453) pointed out in their analysis of field social work function, 'team cohesiveness in terms of values and attitudes was an important element in psychological support and in enabling the work to get done. Dissension between team members was rarely resolved effectively and certainly not within the context of group discussion.' Indeed, the authors found a sort of group conspiracy to negate the importance of conflicts that might otherwise become uncontrollable.

Many writers, including Yalom (1958) and Douglas (1978), recognize that group membership demands specific skills from its participants if groups are to function effectively and achieve both their explicit and implicit goals. In the sense in which we are talking, these context skills are analogous to the competencies that McClelland and Burnham (1976) have described. For McClelland and Burnham competencies are not aspects of a specific job, but are characteristics of the people doing the job best. They reflect the motives, traits, and social skills of workers that are important determinants of the level of performance of specific job-related skills. In the field of human relations training and client welfare, these competencies, or social skills related to improving the effectiveness with which staff perform their primary task, are in many senses intimately related to the therapeutic skills demanded of staff. Training for team-work competency will inevitably also reinforce other training programmes (some of which take place within its own framework) that concentrate on developing contact skills.

Douglas (1978), describing the characteristics of team work, suggests that the decision-making capacity of groups hinges on the process whereby they endorse or reflect the opinions, ideas, and suggestions of constituent members. Implicit in this description is the view that the effectiveness of a team's decision-making capability depends on the extent to which the group is able to accept and welcome new ideas on the part of both new and established staff. It has been recognized for some time that innovation in institutional organizations can be a potent source of anxiety amongst established staff who have already defined for themselves a frame of reference for understanding and performing their tasks based upon the existing order (Jacques 1955; Menzies 1970). Menzies (1970) observed that nursing staff, for example, adopt a wide range of specific behavioural and attitudinal stances to avoid facing, or dealing effectively with both real and anticipated anxiety. Hobbs (1973) has commented on the function of team work being, among other things, to contain work-related anxiety by sharing it amongst many people. Under these conditions there is a greater likelihood of effective strategies being developed if the team is adequately supported. Menzies found that resistance to, or avoidance of, change was one of the patterns adopted by nurses, at both practical and policy level, to cope with overwhelming anxiety.

Pressures to conform in task- and other groups are strong and are clearly of great value in residential settings providing they do not operate to the detriment of creativity and spontaneity. Established treatment programmes need constant monitoring, and, if they are to acquire the skills relevant to organizational goals and not interfere with essential levels of intra-team consistency, new staff need to learn how to implement the prevailing philosophies, policies, and intervention techniques of the establishments they join. One of the problems for residential establishments is to set up support systems for staff that ensure that the maintenance of appropriate levels of conformity and consistency do not topple over into a pattern of dogmatism and inflexibility that would eventually limit a team's effectiveness and cramp the introduction of new ideas that might extend and enrich the quality of life for young people in care.

Douglas's (1978) description of teams gives more clues to the rich complex of forces that operates within such human systems that must be organized and stimulated in order to promote the achievement of team goals. Teams, says Douglas, are human groups that acknowledge membership and the clear value and necessity of shared experience and co-operativeness. As they are quite clearly composed of individuals who implement pro-grammes that usually derive from one specific person (the team leader) and/or organizational policy, they represent a mid-stage between the individual on the one hand and, on the other, self-directing groups. The co-operativeness that must characterize team work is based upon an amalgam of high levels of support and creativity. Groups in this sense do not therefore create new initiatives as an individual would, but rather endorse, accept, modify, or reject the ideas of specific individuals.

The contributions of individual team members can then become the catalyst for developing, modifying, or expanding subsequent inputs from colleagues. This sequential process of expansion of ideas and refinement of thinking has been referred to more explicitly in other fields as brainstorming, although in the normal course of group activity such conscious attention to process may not be particularly apparent.

FURTHER EXPERIENCES OF TEAM WORK

The emphasis for team work and for co-workers in activities involving treatment and human relations to be trained together can be found in a number of sources. The quality of team cohesiveness that Douglas refers to, and which is so important to the effective implementation of any treatment programmes in residential establishments, is one that is comprised of a number of skills and characteristics. Rubenstein and Weiner (1975), evaluating the effectiveness of co-therapy and team work in family therapy, concluded that a major requirement of team work is the capacity to feel that one can rely on, and predict, the behaviour of a colleague in a positive, co-operative fashion, and that one is not working alone but has constructive help available. In short, to trust one's colleagues. Rubenstein and Weiner stressed the important benefits of co-therapists each sharing and learning from the skills and experiences of the other, in order to be able to share assumptions (i.e. personal and professional models for understanding, predicting, and modifying behaviour), and to be able to develop common rules for professional behaviour and treatment expertise. Clients, whether families or disturbed young people in care, can make so many demands for professional help and emotional support that on occasion they can overwhelm therapists. Team work, as Hobbs (1973) points out, can help members carry this burden of demands and anxiety by sharing it out amongst a number of people, rather than allowing it to be carried by one person. Team work can help check staff members' emotional reactions to their clients, which may hinder effective treatment, by introducing an element of co-supervision and monitoring of professional skills and personal and professional behaviour. In this way staff can begin to develop a high degree of professional awareness that in turn can stimulate skills in self-monitoring. Rubenstein and Weiner refer to improved objectivity as only one of a number of additional benefits that arise from co-therapy.

The introduction of team nursing in a general hospital setting (Taylor 1979) was undertaken in order both to give nurses experience and training opportunities by moving from a practice of task-oriented care to one of shared responsibility for several aspects of patient care, and to give nurses the opportunity to acquire a more complete view of their patients. Task-oriented nursing was seen as a policy that inhibited the provision of continuous, consistent care, and that did not promote a sense of being cared for by any specific nurse or nurses. It left patients carrying their own unvoiced anxieties. It was hoped that team nursing would demonstrate that 'nursing staff prefer [it] because they feel more involved with their patients and more directly responsible for their welfare' (Taylor 1979 : 22–3). The outcome of the exercise was that nurses preferred this method of working; that for some it became possible to develop better nurse-patient relationships; that it made it easier to learn the nursing task; and that it afforded nurses more experience in organization and decision making. As a result of introducing team-nursing techniques, many nurses felt that patients had more confidence in the nursing staff.

In the field of human relations training, where much learning is undertaken in a group situation that is facilitated by two or more co-workers, the characteristics of effective intervention by co-operative co-workers have been described as presenting to clients a choice of behavioural and attitudinal models upon which to develop more effective coping behaviours; the pacing of interventions; mutual supervision of professional skills, competence, and performance; and the presentation to clients of a picture of effective interpersonal relationships through both the formal and informal processes of modelling (Pfeiffer and Jones 1975).

Team work in social services teams can be improved by allowing participatory management techniques to be implemented, which lead to greater involvement in the decision-making process for as many staff as possible, in order to increase the likelihood of consensus over important issues and to provide a forum for questioning decisions in a manner that ensures that the whole process can be constantly examined and refined, and can become more sensitive and representative (Briers 1981).

FACTORS AFFECTING THE SUCCESS OF RESIDENTIAL TEAM WORK

There are a number of factors that can limit effective team-work practice. These include educational preparation of staff; role ambiguity and incongruous expectations; status differentials; authority and power structures; leadership styles (Hunt 1981); role confusion; unrealistic aims and the influence of new team members; communication problems; using the task primarily to bolster one's own self-esteem; the influence of client difficulties upon team behaviour (Menninger Foundation Staff 1971); the effect of inappropriate group role behaviour (Reilly 1974); problems with containing anxiety (Menzies 1970); and conflict between different sets of assumptions or models about how to achieve team tasks. We can look at some of these issues here, as some are dealt with elsewhere in the text.

(1) Educational backgrounds and conflict of assumptions

Staff who work together in a team have not necessarily been trained together. Indeed, it is extremely unlikely that this will have happened. Each team member will bring to the work situation a different set of professional values, opinions, skills, and theoretical standpoints, debate about which can drain off vital staff time and energy (that should be available for the client group) in managing excessive levels of interpersonal and professional conflict, unless the organization is organized and motivated so that adequate time can be provided for staff to share, exchange, and explore the variety of viewpoints that exist. Better understanding and consensus can be arrived at in this way.

(2) Role confusion

The use of the term 'team work' implies that individuals within the team are functionally interdependent and are agreed upon a course of action in pursuit of common goals. Where responsibility for tasks is shared, rather than narrowly defined on the basis of training backgrounds, communication problems can arise if the manner of task sharing is not clearly discussed, and if there are 'serious perceptual descrepancies' (Hunt 1981) amongst staff about role behaviour expectations. Each person can be viewed as having an area of skill and expertise that is crucial to the success of the team (Menninger Foundation Staff 1971). Successful team practice must be able to define and acknowledge the importance of these contributions lest staff feel isolated and undervalued. Some, or even many, of these skills may not be specified merely by reference to a person's professional background. Many non-teachers may have high potential for successfully participating in the educational process in residential establishments, whilst the informal efforts of teaching staff may add a richness to a therapeutic programme through an intuitive and sensitive approach to counselling young people in distress. Other role behaviours that need to be clarified in order to improve an understanding by the team of the notion of mutual interdependent contribution may include supportive behaviour, where skills of empathy and listening are employed, perhaps by specific individuals to help others through critical periods in their work with young people, and skills in articulating problems and formulating them in a manner that makes their presentation and discussion acceptable and, hopefully, constructive for the team. Specific individuals may well be identified with these various activities, which may depend upon unique blends of personal skills, professional training, and interests. The wide variety of talents in the area of interpersonal functioning needs to be inventoried and shared if their value to team-work practice is to be understood and valued.

(3) Unrealistic aims and difficulties in sharing and containing anxiety

The impression that the personal conflicts of the seriously disturbed patient can have on the morale of staff can be so great that they either avoid the issue by adopting a series of behavioural and attitudinal defences that are supported by some of the formal organizational structures, or they can experience anxiety based upon an inappropriate assessment of their own skills (in the sense that they devalue their talents) so that they develop stress reactions that can have profound effects on the energies and morale of the team and indeed the client group. This pattern of problems is discussed in more detail in the next chapter in relation to 'worker burn-out'.

(4) Communication problems and unresolved conflicts

As we have seen, some practice teams have attempted to deal with team problems simply by not talking about them. However, unresolved issues inevitably build up a residue of tension and hostility that in turn can distort other aspects of normal team process and complicate the meaning of other pertinent intra-team communication. At a change-over, for example, disagreements about day-to-day child-care practices may be fuelled by feelings that stem from unrelated experiences, say of competition with the leader. Sinclair (1971) found that if staff relationships were characterized by acted-out conflict, staff could become overtly competitive and undermine each other to the extent that the energy that should have been injected into care programmes for residents was absorbed in inappropriate levels of team dispute. Other problems that give rise to communication problems within teams may include deficits in basic communication skills, discrepancies of understanding that occur when staff from different backgrounds use special language and jargon (Menninger Foundation Staff 1971), and cultural divisions between workers.

Cultural splits between residential care workers and senior staff in management teams have been shown to lead to staff splits that are characterized by staff identifying with the values and attitudes of young people in care, and utilizing anti-social factors of the resident's subculture to preserve control, which tended in turn to reinforce clients' anti-social behaviour (Polsky 1963). Polsky also found that in his study residential staff had more in common with clients than senior staff and so recreated anti-authority splits that served only to strengthen the young peoples' attitudes to both the community in general and social factors in the organization that they saw as instrumentally geared to changing their behaviour.

Tensions within staff teams, if not resolved, can be projected back onto the client group and can lead to periods of exaggerated patient disturbance (Stanton and Schwartz 1954). Such tensions need not arise solely from problems relevant in the process of team work but may be engendered by external factors. Poor physical conditions, rigid management hierarchies, and other organizational factors may impinge on team effectiveness (Menninger Foundation Staff 1971). Reports of high levels of emotional and physical disturbance amongst staff may reflect that in some cases staff bring to the teams personal problems that they hope to solve in the climate of help geared to the task of resolving human pain and needs (Miller and Gwynne 1972).

New team members bring specific problems to the team that are related to levels of experience or simply to their being a newcomer (Menninger Foundation Staff 1971). Confusion about roles and mutual expectations may lead to over concern with their own needs by newcomers and by the experienced staff whose energies are drawn out in supportive actions. New members may also be a threat to a team, being composed either of unknown talents that may outstrip those of the team or of deficits that will have to be made good. As we shall show in the chapter on team exercises, new members may thus become a target for projected feelings that currently exist in the team. How to nurture new members of staff is an issue with which teams should be concerned.

(5) Feedback patterns and role confusion

Individuals in teams need to feel confident and secure enough in their own role to disagree with the views of the team. Menninger Foundation Staff (1971) comment that unjustified conformity to individual or group opinion can mean that the full benefits of team work are not being realized. Each person has an area of skill that is vital to the team's success as a work group and if this is to be integrated fully then a clear understanding of both the formal and informal roles within the group, and the manner in which these are productivly brought together, must be a central focus for training and development. Reilly (1974), continuing the description of dysfunctional personal roles, has identified some characteristic role behaviour that is less than useful to successful goal accomplishment. Some disruption of task performance by anxiety may be necessary for growth, but the regular use of the defensive characteristic will, eventually, seriously interfere with team business (Menzies 1970; Stevenson 1977).

A further factor that can influence team performance is the

style of feedback about the level of team effectiveness. Whilst it is commonly held that collective action results in far superior performances than those summed from the efforts of individuals, there is evidence that under certain circumstances group performance may be less effective (Latané 1979). Latané's theory of social impact states that the effect of outside social influences on a group has a diminished effect on individual members, with increasing group size and strength. The effect of this is that some members do not work to capacity if relieved of this outside pressure, and when working in a group, people may feel that any praise or blame is contingent upon the group rather than individual performance. In this way people can either avoid negative feedback by 'hiding in the group', or feel that their positive efforts are not sufficiently recognized. An apparently equal division of credit amongst team members who in fact make differential contributions to the team does not adequately reflect these contributions in the way that is maximally rewarding to the individual. Some members may even 'coast' on group effort. Organizational techniques geared to improving team effectiveness must acknowledge a balance of feedback between what is appropriate for the team and what is beneficial for the development of individual performance and personal self-esteem.

(6) Leadership styles

One of the most significant factors in determining team effectiveness is the impact of the leader. There is a vast literature now available on leadership styles which we cannot summarize here. Menninger Foundation Staff (1971), for example, make some valuable points about the psychological climate created by leaders. Leadership is a function of group cohesiveness and co-operativeness as well as being rooted in the qualities of the leader. An analysis of style needs to reflect both these factors. A dogmatic forceful leader may provoke resentment that inhibits good performance, engenders a sense of not being heard, and a deterioration of commitment to the notion of collective responsibility for achievement. Permissive leaders may not direct a team sufficiently, and one who is anxious about making unpopular decisions, especially if the group's affection for the leader is too strong, may make the process of effective decision making increasingly difficult to implement. The importance of attending to appropriate leadership styles is highlighted by Menninger Foundation Staff (1971) when they say that such inappropriate behaviour may lead to the positive skills and ideas of these leaders being lost in the confusion, resentment, or apathy that they engender.

(7) Blocks to change

Change implies re-definition of roles, and may create considerable anxiety for staff members who have become comfortable within a well-established *modus operandi*. Groups may also be highly resistant to the notion that skills for working in teams can be, or need to be, learned. They can also be resistant to the idea that observation of others is a vital part of the process of learning about behaviour because the need to recognize and acknowledge the experience of group pressure is felt to be a personal affair.

Acknowledgement and a full appreciation of the interplay of these problems in the development of team characteristics, and in the planning of strategies to facilitate team change, are vital if this area of staff training is to succeed.

ORGANIZATIONAL DEVELOPMENT AND TEAM BUILDING

The term 'organizational development' refers to a broad approach to the appraisal and renewal of organizational structure and dynamics and involves the following: an action-research approach (Rubin 1972) covering either the whole organization or a coherent sub-system of the establishment; a long-term initiative, shared by all members of the organization, with the goal of introducing planned change based on a diagnosis of problems; a planned strategy to improve organizational effectiveness and allow for a greater sense of choice, flexibility, and renewal; introducing into the ongoing activities of an organization experiences and learning events that facilitate learning and make more choices available about alternative methods of resolving problems (Sherwood 1972).

Team-building techniques probably constitute one of the single largest components of organizational development techniques, and if a working group is to be seen as a team, and therefore to be appropriately constituted to merit such interventions, then certain criteria have been suggested as being important: the group in question needs clear reasons for working together; members of the group need to be functionally interdependent (that is, they each need the skills and experiences of the others in order to reach mutually agreed goals); team members need to be committed to the concept that co-operative working leads to improved decision making and outcomes; and the group must be recognized, and accountable, as a functioning working unit or system within a larger organizational department (Reilly and Jones 1974).

Residential teams normally meet these criteria. Because of the sheer energy required, the scope of the therapeutic problems, and the range of necessary staff skills that must be made available to institutionalized young people, residential teams have both imposed and self-determined reasons for working together. Staff are functionally interdependent: they rely on the complementary blending of all represented skills in order to meet the various treatment needs of the young people. Also, each member of staff needs to be able to predict the behaviour of other staff as it affects the maintenance of a consistent approach to treatment and the handling of stress arising from confrontation, control, and checking. Each team member must learn to perform in a manner that will enhance the work of others in the team (Menninger Foundation Staff 1971). The diagnostic process of the team involves constant pooling and sharing of information and clinical material, and the integration of data from all staff in order to provide a continually up-dated clinical picture that is an evolving synthesis (as Menninger Foundation Staff call it) depending on continual staff interchange. Teams are normally committed to the notion of co-operative working that involves also a cross-fertilization of skills, experience, and ideas, which, if properly nurtured, will help individual staff cope more ably and effectively with novel or unexpected circumstances. And, of course, residential teams can rightly be considered as sub-systems of a larger organization, be it a training school, a treatment centre, or a social services department.

The goals of team-building programmes

It is widely recognized in all areas of human relations training, and certainly in residential work (Harris and Anderson 1979), that personal and professional differences can create blocks to the effective working of teams that are both painful to endure and, with time, increasingly difficult to confront or resolve. Krause (1974) found that staff in residential treatment establishments differed considerably on a wide range of relevant variables: age, sex, occupational status, pay, experience with children, and educational, social, and cultural backgrounds. Differences in attitude on a range of social and political issues, including those of approaches to child-behaviour management are also found. Such a range of conflicts can contribute to the development of on-site problems. However, by examining and working through these issues in a structured and meaningful way, team building can be organized to improve effective problem solving ability amongst team members.

A number of sub-goals of a team-building experience have been specified (Reilly and Jones 1974) and are worth reviewing in full.

(1) Each team member should come to a deeper understanding of the roles and functions of all team members and the parts those roles play in achieving team goals.
(We should add here that at least as far as residential work is concerned, many roles that are of importance exist independently of professional training, may rely more on personal characteristics and skills, and that each person may well play more than one role.)

(2)   The team should reach an improved comprehension of its purpose and role within the total organization.

(3)   An improved level of communication amongst team members about the real issues that impede the efficiency of the group (e.g. the disclosure of hidden agendas) should be aimed at.

(4)   Greater levels of interpersonal trust and support amongst colleagues need to be achieved.

(5)   A clearer understanding of group behaviour, especially where members work closely and sometimes intimately together, is desirable. In this respect, the effect of role behaviour on group effectiveness, and that of group pressure on individuals to adopt certain roles, are clear targets for the training programme.

(6)   More effective ways of working through problems inherent to the team in both work and personal issues are important.

(7)   The ability to use conflict in a constructive and positive fashion is a vital component of good team work.

(8)   Improved levels of co-operativeness and decreased competitiveness which can be expensive for the individual, the team, and the parent organization need to be seen as targets for training.

(9)   An increased ability to work co-operatively with other sub-groups or teams within the organization is important.

(10) A greater sense of interdependence amongst team members will add to co-operativeness, team work, and effectiveness.

Lest it appear from this and the following chapter that such an approach is too staff-oriented, it should be recalled that one major factor that influences the learning process in children is the process of observation and modelling of the behaviour of others. For young people in care their main day-to-day reference models will be staff. There is a wealth of evidence that young children do modify their behaviour through observing the actions of significant others, especially those in a position of authority (Bandura and Walters 1963), and those who control access to things that are meaningful, desirable, and significant for them. Consciously or otherwise, staff present to young people in care patterns of negotiating interpersonal contact, maintaining rewarding interpersonal relationships, and the performance of a wide range of social skills pertinent to normal living. There should be some congruence between the skills and values that staff try to impart to the children's group as an intentional function of treatment and the observed competence in parallel skills that staff demonstrate during the course of their work. There is evidence that discrepancies between the verbal and non-verbal behaviour of counsellors can affect the outcome of the helping process (Graves and Robinson 1966).

ACTION STRATEGIES AND CONCLUDING REMARKS

The final direction taken by the training programme will be a product of the interplay of the team's personal and professional resources, the issues that need to be confronted, and the success with which each issue is tackled during the course of the programme. However, some specific techniques lend themselves well to such an experience and are certainly indicated by our previous discussion. These strategies include the skills necessary to give and receive constructive personal feedback, negotiation of conflict, the development of high levels of empathic skills (that is, the capacity to understand the communication, feelings, and personal world views held by others), the ability to exchange and modify personal assumptions, and the ability to model effective social skills in a manner that is beneficial for participants and others.

The team-building goals as laid down by Reilly and Jones (1974) include both interpersonal and structural goals. By structural we refer to the formal framework in which the team functions: team and organizational policy on treatment, specific areas of policy development (for example, how therapeutic group meetings and counselling programmes are perceived and implemented), patterns of formal decision making and information transmission (how staff meetings, case conferences, and changeovers function, for example), and the maintenance of all other formal systems that are essential to the healthy functioning of the residential establishment (for example, the concept of key workers, imposed boundaries of treatment responsibility, shift systems, and the definition of leadership responsibilities and tasks). An effective team-training experience should have an appropriate balance of content in respect of these areas of personal and structural aspects, although specific programmes are tailored to the needs and current levels of functioning, in terms of skills and achievements, of each individual team.

5 Team-Building Programmes

The simple assumption that provides the rationale for team development programmes is that if a team works together more effectively then the team will achieve its primary organizational goals more efficiently. In the case of residential care with young people, these goals will encompass the outcomes of treatment and rehabilitation strategies. There is a further benefit accruing to team-building programmes in the fields of health and welfare: the skills to be developed in teams are also those that directly influence the quality of interaction between staff and residents, that is, communication, feedback, problem solving, conflict negotiation, monitoring of interpersonal behaviour, and the containment of anxiety. Team-building strategies can fundamentally affect the climate of relationships and task performance in work teams coping with what Hunt (1981) calls 'interdependent activities'.

Establishing formal team-building programmes that have the explicit goal of helping real-life work teams to diagnose and resolve more effectively the problems that impair their level of functioning is a relatively new departure in staff training. In this approach the work-related behaviour of the team becomes the primary focus for training, held together as it is by both structural and personal factors that define the team. The knowledge and skills that are required to manage team-work conflicts cannot be assumed to be held by team members who are inevitably employed and bound up in their primary tasks of caring for children. Activities that enable team members to set about resolving team problems will need a more or less explicit educational input into a training module, the establishment of which we describe below.

THE IMPLEMENTATION OF TEAM-BUILDING PROGRAMMES

Training programmes are composed of five discrete stages:

(1) Organizational and team commitment
(2) Individual interviews
(3) Planning action interventions and strategies
(4) Feedback and implementation
(5) Evaluation

(1) Organizational and team commitment

Prior to any training experience it is essential that potential participants agree to their involvement. This stage of seeking a consensus of team members at all management levels involves the presentation of the conceptual framework and anticipated goals of the programme, followed by discussion in which participants can question and challenge assumptions and clarify their perceptions of the activities in which they are about to become involved. How easily this stage is resolved will depend on the characteristics of previous levels of functioning within the team. Gilmore *et al.* (1974), in a study of health practice teams, found that problems were most commonly dealt with by a reduction in communication about problem solving and conflict negotiation. That is, in general they avoided the issue by putting a high priority on harmonious relationships, regardless of whether these served a useful team function. There needs, then, to be some real sensitivity to current levels of functioning within teams. Residential teams may feel quite wary of allowing their own work group to become the focus of study, especially if there is some confusion about the differences in personal and professional relationships. Efforts to resolve work-related interpersonal conflicts may then be resisted if a team shows a lack of capacity to resolve conflicts, with the result that staff may feel, consciously or otherwise, that the accumulation of unresolved and painful feelings between staff has become so great that its examination may disrupt the team beyond a level of repair. Presenting the elements and goals of the training programme will have to be tailored to what is known about the team's current level of functioning.

(2) Individual interviews

The investment of time and energy in the preparatory stages is essential if the training programme itself is to be of benefit to the team. Programme structure must be based upon a fusion of the expectations and expressed wishes of team members and the knowledge of the parameters that make for sound interdependent co-operativeness. Staff expectations about the content of the forthcoming programmes can be clarified by a series of individual meetings between the outside consultant to the team and each team member. (Pfeiffer and Jones (1975) refer to these meetings as 'sensing interviews'.) This stage enables team members to clarify and specify the nature of the problems that face the team, and allows for a detailed insight into the specific working of the team involved. Each separate interview helps the consultant to cross-check and validate the views expressed by individuals and to arrive at a clear view of the fundamental issues facing the team. At the same time, each person has a right to his or her own views and feelings, even if they do not concur with those of colleagues. Indeed, discrepancies may constitute a very real barrier to communication and team work in themselves. Because of the nature of the anxiety that can often surround the open discussion of team conflicts, it is important to establish that these individual meetings are confidential to the extent that the findings from all interviews will be relayed back to the group but individuals can choose for themselves whether to 'own' those feelings in public. In this phase of the programme, the aim is to elicit from each team member information about the barriers to effective co-operative practice that they see, notions about how these problems may be resolved, both in the long term and during the training programme itself (e.g. through role play, workshop discussion groups, specific educational input, and sensitivity exercises), some attempt to clarify the characteristics of the team that should result from effective training, and also some firm indication of the current strengths of the team (i.e. assets that can not only carry the team through stressful periods but can also be drawn upon in the attempt to resolve problems).

Even at this stage of the team-building programme, several crucial processes are appearing and being consolidated. During the interview an issue over the development and nature of inter-personal trust develops as many participants, cautiously or otherwise, will attempt to sound out the consultant's capacity and sensitivity to handle the discussion and to resolve painful issues in a safe but constructive manner during the training exercise. If staff develop a level of trust and rapport with the consultant/facilitator, they will be able to acknowledge openly some of the hidden agendas of the team that have been dealt with either by non-communication or inappropriate negotiation. They will also become aware of the areas in which the team can resolve issues effectively, and, as has been indicated already, the planning interview itself offers a training experience in the diagnosis of team-work problems and possible methods of resolution.

(3) Planning action interventions and strategies

At this stage the information collected in individual staff interviews needs to be analysed for common themes that can form the basis of training exercises, as well as any highlighted discrepancy of views that could interfere with team functioning. In this working through of the rationale, cues about how best the rationale may be examined will be looked for. The net result of this stage of the development programme is the balanced presentation of team problems sorted according to the general weighting given them, and the formulation of a tentative training programme geared to meeting these expressed needs.

(4) Feedback and implementation

This phase is concerned with (a) feeding back to the whole team the analysis and proposed strategies developed in the planning stage (3), and (b) the implementation of the final, agreed programme. Feedback usually occurs in the context of a normal staff meeting prior to the training programme. However, for many organizational reasons, it may have to be the first item on the agenda of the programme proper. The facilitator will give the team his or her findings from the individual interview stage and will make proposals for action. Usually at this stage some relief is felt by the team as they perceive the degree of common feeling about the problems that confront them. A thorough discussion should then occur, aimed at reaching agreement amongst team members about which topics must be discussed and which methods would be most appropriate and acceptable. Everyone should have an opportunity to put their views forward and feel that they are being consulted and involved in the decision-making process; it is essentially their *team*-building training programme that may or may not enable significant positive changes to occur in the diagnosed problem areas. It is in everyone's interests to be listened to and heard.

(5) Evaluation

Problems that concern teams

There are a number of problem areas that are often reported on by residential staff. These relate to

(1) Defining organizational policy and setting realistic goals.
(2) Understanding the contribution of each team member and the role behaviours that are functional or dysfunctional with respect to good teamwork, i.e. team-work process.
(3) Conflict over basic assumptions about the nature and theoretical basis of the treatment process.
(4) The more effective management of interpersonal and inter-professional relationships, e.g. bringing out and resolving hidden agendas, and negotiating conflict.
(5) Improving communication either through the process of experiential skills acquisition or discussion about organizational changes that will allow more time for communication.
(6) The need for appropriate levels of interpersonal sensitivity and support.

At this point some comments about the relationship between the facilitator and the team leader need to be recorded and clarified. As the team leader is of central importance to the team's professional and personal well-being, and is responsible to senior management officials in respect of these areas, it is crucial that his or her normal role *vis à vis* the team is not undermined by the activities and interventions of the facilitator. The leader should be prepared well in advance so that he or she will not hold unrealistic expectations about what can or will be done. Our experience has shown that the team leader and the facilitator must work closely together throughout the five stages of the programme (and ensure that all team members know this), and build in their own suggestions regarding the definition and resolution of problems and programme format. It is important to acknowledge the special role of the leader, his or her overall awareness of group climate that exists in the team, from levels of trust and openness to degree of specific skills and their appropriate allocation. The team leader is, after all, the on-the-spot team-builder, a responsibility formally allocated on appointment.

At the same time, the consultant must emphasize that he or she is working on behalf of the whole team (Bradford 1976) and not just for the team leader or central organizations. In this sense the role of the leader is as valid as any other subject of team-building techniques. We have found that this dilemma can be resolved through the ascription of both an informal and an explicit working relationship between the facilitator and the team leader. Using the model of co-working developed by Pfeiffer and Jones (1975), which emphasizes the benefits of co-therapy as: effective pacing of interventions, mutual support and supervision of levels of professional skills, modelling of effective interpersonal relationships, presentation of a wider choice of behavioural and attitudinal moods upon which members may choose to build personal change, the facilitator and team leader work together as co-facilitators. This style of working, whether at human relations training levels or in family therapy, provides space for each co-worker to attend to specific aspects of the group's development and to ensure that as little material as possible is overlooked. One co-worker can either be an observer of group processes and behaviour, or an active strategist in the sense of participating actively in the emotional life of the group in order to effect change (Rubenstein and Weiner 1976). The specific model of co-working that we have defined determines that the group consultant, or outside facilitator, takes the most active role in the early stages of the group, giving instructions, setting tasks and exercises, and leading role-plays, for example. As the group relaxes and develops the confidence to tackle more pertinent yet painful issues, such as hidden agendas, the two work closely together in what is hopefully a model of shared, co-operative working, a collaborative effort for a more creative type of intervention in which the team leader can sensitively introduce 'emotional' material of which the facilitator may be unaware, and provide a fuller basis for intervention.

This model provides a basis for sharing responsibility for what the group produces both in terms of demands for problem resolution and sharing the burdens of emotional overload from feelings that can often erupt when a group feels free enough to explore more personal issues. Towards the end of the training programme, the team leader takes increasing responsibility for directing the programme, using his or her time to develop specific policy issues that may have arisen during the week or to develop the sense of 'team'. At this point, the outside facilitator can act primarily as an observer of group processes and provide input where needed on knowledge or practice of strategies that might resolve any outstanding issues.

During the training programme, the team leader and facilitator meet regularly, usually after each morning and afternoon session, in order to share their experience and perceptions and to plan any necessary changes in programme format. High levels of trust, respect, and co-operativeness are necessary between consultant and team leader if they are to be able to integrate their personal styles of intervention harmoniously. This implies, and often entails, team leaders in residential establishments being given opportunities for further training in management and team-building techniques.

ISSUES THAT CONFRONT A TEAM

Several consistent themes emerge from interviews with residential staff about perceived team (in)effectiveness. These can be grouped under various headings, but the balance of needs for the team, and the style of intervention shown, may differ depending upon the organizational goals of the team, their complexity, the level of resources and skills both necessary and available, the team's 'age' as an interdependent group, and its previous experience and success at handling inherent team problems.

MISMANAGEMENT AND MANAGEMENT OF STRESSES ON RESIDENTIAL WORKERS

The manner in which residential staff respond to and cope with work-related stress and anxiety has recieved considerable attention in the last few years (see Jacques 1955; Menzies 1970; Maslach 1976; Daley 1979; and Barrett and McKelvay 1980). Some writers have identified the handling of stress as a prominent factor in determining levels of institutional success (e.g. Menzies 1970). Most stress is felt to stem from the necessity of taking risks in the residential situation and making decisions that may have profound and far-reaching consequences for the client, the worker, and even the organization (Walton 1978).

One of the first major studies of how staff cope with work-related anxiety was conducted by Isobel Menzies (1970) who studied the behaviour of nurses working with terminally ill patients. Both Menzies and Elliott Jacques, in his (1957) study of business concerns, have looked at the manner in which the 'social defense system' of an establishment can be defined by reference to the manner in which staff handle stress. Menzies's subjects experienced considerable stress related to the emotional dilemmas of caring for terminally ill patients and they displayed a clear pattern of behaviours and attitudinal stances.

(1) There was a 'splitting' of the nurse-patient relationship, facilitated by an impersonal labelling of patients (e.g. 'the

cancer in bed one'), which prevented nurses becoming too close to the patients.

(2) There was a second, consequential activity in the depersonalization, categorization, or denial of the significance of the individual.

(3) Staff also came to deny their feelings and became emotionally detached from the work content.

(4) A series of checks and rechecks of daily routines, procedures, and tasks served to reduce the weight of responsibility in decision making.

(5) By further ritualizing task performance, or putting an exaggerated emphasis on routine, the need for decision making and risk could be lessened further.

(6) Responsibility and irresponsibility were redistributed socially in a collusive manner and the formal distribution was made purposefully obscure.

(7) Further delegation of responsibility for events, crises, and task completion further lessened the responsibility falling upon staff.

(8) Nurses sometimes coped with perceived or expected anxiety by either idealizing (over-rating) or underestimating their own personal developmental capacities.

(9) A simple measure used to avoid stress was to resist change.

It would be wrong to state simply that these behaviour patterns were unacceptable and implied a value judgement on staff. Rather, they are observations about how staff may react when faced with perceived stress at a high level. Staff have been observed to deliberately subvert the rules of a residential unit in order to add a naturalness in relationships that may seem inhibited by staff-client patterns of interaction that are defined simply according 'to the book' (Millham *et al*. 1978). The impact of a very seriously damaged young person on the high expectations of residential staff in their capacity and skills to effect change can lead to considerable stress and anxiety and feelings of being deskilled and worthless (see Menninger Foundation Staff 1971; Barrett and McKelvay 1980). A tendency to avoid or resist change is a common phenomenon manifested by the difficulties that can greet a member of staff new to a residential team (Menninger Foundation Staff 1971). However, many of these behaviour patterns may generate greater work-related stress and further tension within the social system of the organization. If left unchecked this could lead to the consolidation of an impoverished and maladaptive staff-client culture.

Maslach (1976) argues that the major source of work-related stress is rooted in the context of the interpersonal relationship between residential workers and their clients. The dehumanization of the client also leads to reduced level of staff effectiveness, which further robs the client of the therapeutic skills of staff. Such a defensiveness may well combat anxiety by reducing it to workable levels, but if the anxiety persists or even increases, as it may, when clients continue to make emotional demands on staff, or even increase demands because they see helping staff experiencing a deterioration in performance and capacity to care, then excessive energy may be used in containing escalating levels of stress. In extreme cases such coping mechanisms may become increasingly ineffective and yet even more entrenched if no support is available to the worker to find alternative methods, both at personal and organizational levels to manage experienced stress. Eventually, work performance may deteriorate in an erratic fashion as personal energy is more and more consumed by the need for personal survival. As Maslach (1976: 16) states, 'detachment and resistance give way to exhaustion and a total breakdown characterised by anxiety overload'. Whatever the effect on staff, which can be severe and distressing in extreme cases, profound effects on young people may occur as they see key figures in their lives becoming increasingly demoralized, ineffective, and deskilled; these are the figures whom they are testing to the limit, yet at the same time upon whom they may also desperately depend.

This extreme situation is often referred to as 'burn-out' (Daley 1979; Barrett and McKelvay 1980) and in general terms can have serious consequences for the institution. If young people have put considerable emotional pressure upon staff who collapse or suffer in some way, then their compound reactions, based on their own complex motives for testing staff, could leave them with guilt feelings that are difficult to resolve. They may also hold some distorted expectations about the quality of interpersonal relationships they are able to make and about the possible consequences of those relationships for other people. Therefore, at both staff and treatment levels it is important to recognize the specific signs of this stress reaction so that it can be managed more effectively.

Specific characteristics of burn-out

Staff burn-out is characterized by and experienced as a 'sense of failing, wearing out, becoming exhausted through excessive demands on resources and energy' (Daley 1979: 443). A member of staff who is affected in this way may feel alienated from the task and experience both failing job satisfaction and a deteriorating work performance. The process occurs gradually and is often marked by peaks of tension that can be reduced by periods of rest. On occasions staff may appear to be working very hard, yet achieving little. They may express negative or cynical attitudes towards the organization and young people, and eventually adopt behaviours in the work situation that increasingly remove them from contact with young people, for example, finding lots of things to do in the office (Barrett and McKelvay 1980).

Specific causes of staff exhaustion

The causes of staff exhaustion are far too numerous to draw together here. Daley (1979) and Barrett and McKelvay (1980) have drawn up inventories of factors that collectively can contribute to the syndromes outlined. Such factors can be defined in terms of those arising from (1) *the nature of the staff-client relationship* (Maslach 1976), including violent behaviour, manipulation of staff behaviour and feelings by a young person, role confusion (Menninger Foundation Staff 1971), a disparity between the problems of the client and staff resources available to intervene effectively, experiencing too many crises, and continued dealing with the powerful and painful feelings of young people about their life situation; from (2) *personal factors* which might include work overload, being asked to fulfil too many job roles, or role conflict (staff are asked to perform tasks that may be, or appear to be, mutually incompatible); and from (3) *organizational factors* which might include relationships between staff and with authority, a split between those with authority for making decisions and those with responsibility for carrying them out, having no time to plan treatment instead of simply coping with continuing crises, lack of internal support systems, an overload of work stemming from poor planning or poor staffing levels, and receiving feedback from others only when one's work performance is poor.

HOW CAN STRESS BE MANAGED MORE EFFECTIVELY?

The above discussion indicates a number of areas in which planned change can be made to facilitate the improved management of stress.

(1) Identifying stressful features in a given work environment

At this stage staff should be aided in identifying those factors in the work situation, and if necessary in their own personal lives, that are felt to contribute to the development of work strain. By identifying these points of crisis in the institution, proper training programmes can plan for these contingencies and prepare staff to be better equipped to deal with them. Crisis points may be concerned with a lack of knowledge, skills, or resources to handle specific problems effectively (e.g. an anti-staff client group, an aggressive child, or even intra-team conflicts). Hoghugi (1978) states that the proper focus for planning effective in-service training is the location of critical points in the fabric of the institution and its culture.

(2) Developing strategies for coping with stress

It should be clear by now that the occurences of institutional stress can point to areas of skill deficiency or lack of appropriate planning strategies within the organization as well as problems about personal resources and strengths. Modifying organizational factors such as improving staff-support systems, realistic job distribution, and sharing of cases (Daley 1980), will aid the reduction of burn-out problems, as will the development of team-building programmes where skills of consensus can be taught. Discussion and problem sharing amongst team members have been shown to reduce feelings of guilt and anxiety produced by work situations (Menninger Foundation Staff 1971; Hobbs 1973). States of stress are also composed of physiological components that can be approached through the use of relaxation and bio-feedback techniques (Miechenbaum and Goodman 1971; Karlins and Andrews 1975) that have now been established as methods of enabling people to develop effective self-management skills in the control of various physiological functions related to stress (heart and pulse rate, and skin resistance).

The supervision process in residential care can be used to help staff in the process of job enrichment (Fant and Ross 1979). Pines and Kafrey (1978), in a study of factors associated with staff burn-out in residential establishments (including job characteristics such as task variety, autonomy, work success, job significance, and feedback), established that only feedback was significantly associated with burn-out. In other words, the smaller the amount of feedback, the greater the stress experienced. This is understandable when one considers that in many establishments dealing with highly disturbed young people, job satisfaction in the form of tangible rewards is hard to obtain, as young clients are often neither vocal nor forthcoming and may be in residence against their will; curses, threats, and negation of the skills and contribution of the residential worker to their progress are more likely to occur. It is vital in residential care, especially in long-term care or in situations where young people move on before they finally return to the community, that staff receive some ongoing feedback about their contribution to the treatment process, in order that the maximum meaning can be given to the operational skills that staff develop in the everyday practice of their profession. The supervision process should help staff develop awareness of their skills, strengths, and abilities, and emphasize the need for personal planning and a familiarization with the emotional changes that accompany stressful events (Barrett and Mckelvay 1980).

Not all stress is maladaptive. Indeed, a certain level of anxiety and tension may well serve to stimulate personal growth (Selye 1956; Menzies 1970). In the sense that we have been talking about tension, the focus has been on that level of stress that is debilitating and that exceeds the normal resources of the individual or group to manage it effectively. One of the major benefits of the team-skills training approach is that it helps staff to gain a deeper understanding of team and group processes. One of the benefits of the team approach is that there can be a common sharing of tasks so that other people can take over in particular situations when an individual comes under too much pressure from specific points in the treatment process. Other staff can provide on-the-spot supervision skills in order to help an individual achieve a more realistic level of objectivity about a situation, for example, in the case where a particular staff member begins to react emotionally and unhelpfully when a counselling activity puts him or her in touch with the immense despair, pain, or guilt being experienced by a youngster. Alternatively, a staff member can be allowed to stand back gradually from the stress of continually having to confront or be confronted by a particular child; other staff members can take over this role and offer support through a process of sharing and sensitivity, providing that such a 'changeover' is accomplished without weakening the perceived professional strength of the individual concerned.

EXERCISES AND OUTCOMES

One of the first exercises incorporated into a team-skills programme is one that focuses on improving communication and establishing goals for the team-training exercise as a whole. Staff are asked to pair off, preferably with a team member with whom they feel they may have had no recent significant interaction, and develop notes on the characteristics of an effective residential team. After a short period on this task, pairs are invited to join in groups of four or six (depending on team size) to discuss, share, and sharpen up their proposals. Finally, all sub-groups meet together and task-group findings are printed out on large posters. The list can then be refined until it contains all the valuable comments made. It then exists for the remainder of the team meeting as a yardstick against which the team can measure their ongoing performance as a co-operative team. More explicit use can be made of such findings by asking staff to rate these characteristics in order of their priority of importance for team work, for themselves as team members, and also indicate the opportunities that currently exist in the team culture for the attainment of these goals. Large discrepancies between ratings of priority and opportunity can indicate primary targets for staff training exercises. Indeed, this first exercise may act as a meeting that additionally reaches the skills of reaching consensus over the pressing training needs of the team that will enable people, on the day, to participate in the shaping and direction of the final training programme. Similar exercises can be developed to open up discussion on organizational and team policies, levels and types of residential skills needed in the team, treatment techniques, and the roles of staff. Throughout all these exercises, staff are encouraged to use good communication skills, that is expressing views clearly, listening, confronting in constructive disagreement, and trying to understand the other person's point of view (Danish and Hauer 1977).

As an example, the outcome of exercises forming on the qualities of a good or effective residential team will be described below. Each team that takes part in such exercises develops different notions, depending on the particular nature of the climate of that group at that time. Such an exercise helps further a team's capacity to solve its own problems as a group and to develop an awareness of the signs that team dysfunction is occurring (Bradford 1976). The characteristics of an effective group can be grouped in a number of ways, and for the sake of convenience the following ideas have been categorized under the headings of (1) skills, learning, and supervision; (2) support and responsibility; (3) emotional climate, communication, and awareness; and (4) organizational issues.

(1) Skills, learning, and supervision

    (i) The skills of all team members need to be acknowledged, nurtured, and shared wherever possible.

  (ii) The team must be able to provide a working model of skill and interaction upon which newer staff will have the opportunity to model aspects of their own work behaviour, especially that which needs to be consistent with team policy.

 (iii) A good team will let its members know what they are proficient at, and take full advantage of all the personal and professional strengths of its members.

 (iv) Teams should remain open to examining and incorporating new ideas and skills into their work format and recognize that the disqualification of new staff can lead to an atmosphere that dampens creativity and spontaneity.

  (v) By sharing skills and tasks (and even some role behaviour) on a team basis, team members will be able to compensate for one another at both practical and emotional levels, in order to effectively facilitate the completion of primary tasks.

 (vi) Supervision, both from outside consultants and from other team members, is a training priority for all teams. Intra-team supervision demands a high level of involvement in the care task, and feelings of responsibility amongst team members for preserving and developing their own team ethos. Supervision is vital to help staff keep a perspective on the boundaries between their personal needs and the demands of work; it helps to preserve valuable emotional boundaries between staff and young people and keep them intact by a continual process in which staff prompt each other on the appearance of inappropriate work behaviour, e.g. 'over-involvement', 'distancing', 'cynicism', or anger towards clients, that is not being worked through. Most experienced staff should participate in the supervision process for newer staff, and all members need to recognize that those who can be identified as being in need of supervision may already be feeling emotionally isolated and professionally deskilled. He or she may even see the offer of help through supervision or support as a threat that might expose their weaknesses. Staff must be aware of these potential blocks to supervision and plan accordingly.

(vii) Within the team there should exist a level of respect for the contribution of various disciplines, and there needs to be room for conflict of ideas and values as long as these are discussed openly and non-judgementally.

(2) Support and responsibility

(i) Each team member needs to be able to trust, rely upon, and predict the behaviour of colleagues in areas where co-operative effort is called for.

(ii) Co-operative working is an essential ingredient of team work.

(iii) The development of empathic skills will facilitate mutual understanding.

(iv) If staff are tolerant of one another then differences in outlook can be incorporated into the team approach.

(v) The team needs to recognize that under certain circumstances individuals may need to retreat from the emotional pressures of residential work.

(vi) An atmosphere of trust, understanding, and sensitivity must be created if continuity in care is to be allowed for by accepting (v). There also needs to be the notion of interchangeable roles within the team.

(vii) In order for staff to communicate effectively, they must create real opportunities for doing so.

(viii) The team must recognize that it will change with every new member but that it will remain a 'safety net' in which new staff can make mistakes in safety and continue to receive feedback that will promote personal growth.

(ix) The structure and culture of the team should provide a

safe place for the resolution of intra-team conflicts, and for the development of appropriate skills, including the acceptable expression of painful feelings.

(x) With help from outside consultants where necessary, the team should be more capable than any individual within it of dealing effectively with anxiety, frustration, and guilt as reactions to the pressures of working with difficult and disturbed young people.

(xi) Team members must be aware of the effect that the personal characteristics of a sub-team and the behaviour of young people can offer one another.

(3) Emotional climate, communication, and awareness

(i) An effective residential team should recognize the blocks to effective communication and feel capable of discussing, sharing, and resolving work-related hidden agendas. The presence of intra-team conflicts should be acknowledged, and staff should take responsibility for resolving them.

(ii) A good team recognizes the need for team members to validate one another by giving effective interpersonal feedback.

(iii) Individuals need to be honest within their communication with colleagues, listening effectively to, and showing respect for, the views of others in a non-judgemental fashion.

(iv) The team needs to appreciate the dynamics that shape the life of the team, including the constructive and destructive aspects of group pressure on individual behaviour and the effect of individual behaviour on group effectiveness.

(v) In this respect, the behaviour of the staff team may also be influenced by the dynamics and specific treatment problems of the young people. Staff awareness of group process could add to our appreciation of the acting out behaviour of the young people's group.

(vi) The behavioural characteristics of individuals in team interactions provide formal and informal, conscious and unconscious, opportunities for staff to model appropriate (or inappropriate) interpersonal skills to young people.

(4) Organization and policy

  (i) The team must have united aims, which can be achieved if there is constant communication, and a commitment by all staff to the residential task.

 (ii) Work methods must be capable of being updated and renewed where possible. Staff should feel confident enough to explore new working methods.

(iii) Organizational policy on treatment and child-care practice should be clear, consistent, and comprehensible and capable of being translated into effective day-to-day activity. All staff should be aware of all policy and organizational goals.

Useful discussion usually follows on from such an exercise and this can ease people into thinking more clearly and openly about the problems of the team. Staff can find time throughout the training exercise to check out individual feelings and reactions on these issues with other people. In the next chapter we will look more specifically at some of the exercises and processes that can be utilized to facilitate the team-building experience. It is important to reiterate that such an approach must not become an end in itself; team-building exercises are for the ultimate benefit of young people in our care. If intra-team or organizational conflict exists then everyone loses out, but no one more so than the young people whose worst expectations about 'caring adults' could be confirmed by those who should have been most dependable.

6 Team-Building Exercises

In this chapter we look at some of the exercises and processes that can be used in team-building training programmes. The order of the exercises is not specific as each programme must be tailored to the individual needs of teams involved. For some teams the content may even be primarily educational in nature, using lectures and workshops to discuss themes on the techniques of residential care, or it may be a combination of educational input plus experiential exercises. This chapter focuses on some of the experiential aspects of team training. We should point out that such programmes do not turn out totally well-adjusted teams. Conflict and tension are built into the nature of residential work and these programmes are geared both to trying to resolve some outstanding issues for the team and at the same time to trying to help the team deal more effectively and more immediately with on-the-job issues as they arise. It is important that the exercises are carried out in an atmosphere of acceptance and warmth, although tense periods will often occur. Respect for the capacity of individuals to learn is vital; people must not be talked down to but encouraged to articulate themes for themselves as groups (i.e. the themes that confront them). Long-term evaluation of this approach is still needed, but initial experiences are encouraging.

COMMUNICATION SKILLS

Good team-work competency can also facilitate a broad-based assessment of young people's needs and behaviours in a wide range of social situations and interpersonal interactions in a manner that might well be missed by the more isolated worker. The capacity to collate and integrate clinical information about the attitudes and behaviour of young people is a vital precursor to effective treatment. It demands not only good skills in observation and assessment, but also lines of interpersonal communication amongst team members who are aware of the personal, social, and clinical blocks to communication that can arise in a clinical setting.

Team-building training exercises can help in these areas by providing opportunities to improve team communication. Discussion, workshops, and role plays can help to highlight the effect of blocks to communication and improve the openness and trust amongst team members. All these exercises will need to focus on the conditions that impede good communication: hostility between members, emotional blocks (which may reflect idiosyncratic responses to the dilemmas and demands of the residents), hidden agendas, defensiveness, status within the group, inarticulateness, stereotyping, past experiences of communication within a particular team setting, the nature of the specific relationships between team members, and charisma and preoccupation (Pfeiffer 1973). Exercises can be arranged in sequence so that they introduce more threatening or more complex situations in a more manageable fashion. Our first exercises are simply ones for promoting discussion within pairs, then small groups, and then finally in a large group setting. Participants are encouraged to get others to put their points clearly and simply, to check that they have heard what others meant to say and that they themselves have been correctly understood. The content of such exercises can also vary from organizational issues to those that represent more threatening issues about the emotional life of the team as a clinical task force. Team policy and goals, and the specification of skills and staff resources that are available in the staff group, or that need to be made available in the staff group, or that need to be made available for further training, in order to provide the necessary levels of treatment, care, and control, are all valid subjects for such exercises (which can thus set a dual goal of improving team communication, and goal-setting techniques), as are the more painful issues of articulating the emotional effects upon individuals and the staff group, of working with damaged and disturbing young people. Such groups can provide a basis for openness and sharing that, in a properly conducted group, can reduce defensiveness and feelings of isolation that are all too common even in the best team. We will see that one of the tasks of such exercises can be to develop profiles of the characteristics of effective residential teams. Another task can be to examine the effect of a range of hidden agendas, that is themes and preoccupations that affect the significant life of the group, but which members might be reluctant to reveal for fear of anticipated consequences, which may range from rejection by the group to the disorganization of the team's working capacity.

Such an exercise requires team members to role-play a staff meeting or sub-team changeover. Moreover, each team member brings to the exercise an undisclosed hidden agenda of his or her choice. The remainder of the group observes the role-play and tries to establish both the nature of the agendas that are covertly influencing the meeting, and their effect on communication, morale, and, eventually, treatment effectiveness. Such exercises are often enjoyable and are almost invariably dramatic as the group faces real issues in the training room context. Two examples of agendas that team members can choose are competitiveness with the leader or with another sub-team, and acute anxiety provoked by a painful and intense contact with a young person at a point of crisis for themselves (leading possibly to preoccupation, irritability, and even anger over suggested methods of child management that less involved staff may suggest). Wood (1977) described five factors leading to effective interpersonal communication: self-concept; listening; clarity of expression; coping with angry feelings; and self-disclosure. Development of these skills must also be a valid focus for study in team building. People's attitudes towards themselves have a powerful influence on their capacity and willingness to communicate to others on significant issues and on their capacity to accept criticism of a constructive nature or to express their feelings. Lack of self-esteem can block off an individual from the very experiences that could improve the lack; team-building programmes must develop an atmosphere in which members can feel accepted and respected by others for their value to the team. Whilst lack of self-esteem should not be a dominant problem for mature residential staff, the effect of working with disturbed and manipulative young people whose behaviour often seems so deeply entrenched as to be unmodifiable by available resources, or who can be skilful at making hurtful comments about one's weakest areas of personal functioning, can make this an essential ongoing focus for help and intervention.

Team-work programmes must provide opportunities for members to learn the skills of listening and clearly expressing their own feelings if they are to make a realistic improvement in team-work skills. For many people such goals can be quite threatening, especially if imposed on an existing organizational structure that has developed defences for dealing with work-related anxiety. These exercises will inevitably involve individuals in risk-taking and conflict negotiation. Exercises that can bring into the team's awareness the skills needed for effectively challenging others and oneself over a variety of issues and themes should be built into such staff training. In other exercises usually conducted early on in the programme, individuals are asked to pair off and share with one another an area of behaviour or interaction within the team where taking a risk (i.e. trying out a new behaviour) may have positive outcomes both for themselves and others. This may involve asking a significant person for feedback about behaviour in given circumstances (e.g. 'Am I someone you rely on at work or are you unsure about my responses to the children?'), or confronting someone about inappropriate behaviour they have shown on duty. Taking risks, especially in a team situation where staff know each other and are dependent upon one another, may well involve confrontation, a term normally associated with negative, emotionally painful experiences that most people would rather avoid. However, this should be far from the truth. Egan (1975) defined confrontation as the actions of one person that lead another to examine, reflect upon, question, or change some aspect of their behaviour. Staff should also be sensitive to the fact that confrontation will mean different things to different people, and, similarly, that different staff will be affected variably by a range of issues. The open sharing of positive, sensitive, and tender feelings in a group may be very threatening to an introvert team member and some people may find it painful to talk about team behaviour that is negative and destructive, such as backbiting and cynicism, in case it should damage the morale of the team. This is not to say that these responses are appropriate or otherwise; rather, staff should be aware that they may have significant meaning for individuals. To deal with the set of problems outlined above, specific exercises, or inputs to group discussions in the sense of how members might better relate to one another, can be implemented. Feedback exercises can help to establish conditions in the group in which individuals may feel more accepted and self-confident and hence more receptive to the benefits of communications exercises and exercises involving the negotiation of conflict and risk-taking.

A useful exercise for teams new to this training technique is the 'feedback silhouette'. Staff trace out on newsprint fixed to a wall the outline of all other members, who, in turn, display on their own silhouette a brief synopsis of their interests, hobbies, and professional skills. All group members are then told that they can write work-related comments, which give feedback on how one person sees another, on other people's silhouettes. However, team members are cautioned to ensure that in so doing they follow the guidelines for giving constructive feedback. These skills have been described by various authors, for example Kurtz and Jones (1973), Hanson (1975), and Bradford (1976). It should be possible to minimize an individual's defensiveness and improve their capacity to use feedback and criticism constructively. Accurate feedback is of little use or benefit from someone too anxious to receive it, and skills in giving feedback point to ways of helping individuals listen more productively. These issues are developed at greater length in other sources but can be summarized as follows. Feedback is more effective if (i) feelings are expressed directly; (ii) it concerns observable, describable behaviour rather than interpretation of motives; (iii) it is non-evaluative in nature (i.e. it refers to behaviour rather than 'good' or 'bad' judgements of personal worth); (iv) it is directed towards specific aspects of an individual's behaviour that is also capable of being modified; (v) the recipient of the feedback is left feeling free to choose whether or not to act; (vi) constructive feedback is as immediate as possible; (vii) it is asked for rather than imposed; and if (viii) those who are giving feedback are motivated to be helpful and constructive rather than hurtful. Clearly, in this exercise feedback is being given rather than being requested, and the group should ensure that opportunities are created for individuals to ask for feedback. These skills, if properly guided and developed, can then help the team develop the sort of group atmosphere that Kurtz and Jones (1973) say is conducive to effective negotiation of conflict: the establishment of good interpersonal relationships between those involved; the development of sensitivity to the needs of others in those who confront; when there is an atmosphere in which members accept and respect each other and are willing to get involved with each other; when confrontations are phrased as requests and suggestions rather than as demands; and when those who confront are capable of distinguishing effectively between facts, feelings, and theories. Kurtz and Jones also say that particular skills to be developed in those who receive feedback (who are confronted) are the willingness and capacity to tolerate the anxiety that can stem from the temporary degree of personal disorganization that can occur as one's self-concept undergoes some modification, and the ability to respond differently, rather than in a stereotyped manner, to different types of confrontation.

At some stage during the programme, individuals in the team or even the whole group may request that interpersonal feedback be given more directly, perhaps even in the large group setting. Several strategies are available here, depending on the facilitator's assessment of the strength of the group and its members to cope with such experiences. For example, individuals may be instructed to seek out other individuals or groups in order to give or solicit feedback about themselves or others in the work situation. Another strategy entails staff completing questionnaires about specific aspects of behaviour in groups (e.g. how to lead a therapeutic group with clients) or with respect to another person (i.e. completing such an inventory by reflecting how they see another person in that situation). This material can then be used for discussion in pairs, followed by a more general large group workshop on the themes that emerged. A third, more sensitive, and threatening technique is for members to solicit feedback about themselves in a large group. This can be done in a number of ways but the following have proved particularly useful. Using a given working situation as the focus for discussion, such as the confrontation by staff of a violent child, or a staff member's approach to a child who is depressed, the team can generate for each individual member the way in which they anticipate the staff member will react in that situation. These views can be examined for both the variability of perceptions of an individual held by others, and the discrepancy between these views and those of the member of staff concerned. Such an exercise can provide two-way, interpersonal, work-related feedback; not only does the individual have to come to terms with the views held by others, but also the rest of the group will be able, in discussion, to appreciate more of an individual's confidences, anxieties, and personal notions of behaviour management and treatment (Leventhal and Slemburg 1977). The exercise can facilitate an improvement in understanding between staff.

Another technique involves each team member asking for both a positive comment upon and a constructive criticism of their work behaviour from each of the other team members. Because it can be threatening, this exercise should be used with caution. It should only be carried through if all participants agree and it is best done in an atmosphere of trust, openness, and sharing, characteristics of a group that may take some time to develop to maturity.

ROLE BEHAVIOURS IN GROUPS

Reilly and Jones (1974) point to the importance of staff members of a work team being aware of the effect of functional and dysfunctional role behaviours upon group performance and success, and the effect of group pressures and dynamics as they influence and shape the development of certain role behaviours. Two role-play and workshop exercises have proved especially useful in helping staff to become more conscious of, and therefore potentially more in control of, the stances that can influence the success or failure of team work. These exercises have been adapted from human relations training formats described by Pfeiffer and Jones (1972–80).

Exercise one

This exercise examines the effect of individual behaviour patterns upon group outcome and, in particular, leadership behaviour. In recent years considerable attention has been given to defining the nature, characteristics, and determinants of leadership behaviour in groups. Menninger Foundation Staff (1971) have pointed to dysfunctional leadership styles as an important determinant of the breakdown of team-work effectiveness. Carter *et al.* (1968) and Fiedler and Korton (1968) have described how certain situational factors develop to produce shifts between democratic and autocratic styles of leadership. There tends to be a shift from democratic towards autocratic leadership when either the methods for attaining group goals are ambiguous or unclear, or where, in situations where the attainment of goals is considered to be more important than the attainment of individual goals, the need to satisfy individual drives begins to predominate. Reilly and Jones (1964) have described some specific behavioural roles that can have destructive effects on group processes. Amongst these are the dominator, the side-tracker, the saboteur, the clown, the competitor for leadership, and the cynic. The behaviour patterns displayed by the group members occupying these roles can have the effect, consciously or otherwise, of disrupting effective group behaviour as well as serving to satisfy the personal agendas of individual participants, e.g. becoming the centre of attention, distracting the group away from legitimate issues that may prove too painful for individuals to discuss, or discrediting or usurping the leader. These behaviours can only continue to meet personal needs at the expense of group competence. When groups meet to perform legitimate tasks, they must be trained to recognize, amongst other things, the need for taking responsibility for their own behaviour. First of all, however, they have to recognize it. This exercise, like many others, has any number of variations, and only two will be described here.

In the first variation, volunteers for a role-play exercise each collect a role and a behavioural description from the trainer. These instructions are typed on a card and each member keeps their own counsel over the role they are to play. After being given some time to think themselves into their roles, which have been given out at random, the group members are asked to convene and spend some time in role-play discussing a value-laden topic such as the limits to put on the smoking behaviour of children in their care. The group is then told that someone amongst them is to play the part of a democratic group leader. The leader has been instructed to counsel the views of all members, to try to ensure that they feel listened to and that they have participated actively in the decision-making process, and to try to ensure that individuals are given some opportunity to meet their own needs constructively. The group is told to reach substantial agreement about the issue in question. Some of the roles that can be given to other members include, in addition to those mentioned earlier, the silent person, the intellectualizer, and the effective group member (as a stimulus for later discussion about appropriate group behaviour). The role-play is dominated by participants with a range of goals and agendas, many of which are antipathetic to the stated group goal, or at least the process by which that is to be most effectively reached.

The outcome of this exercise, which is invariably enjoyable, is that most participants occupying the role of democratic leader exhibit a clear shift of leadership style, often within a short period, say twenty minutes into the role play. This is demonstrated by a developing preference for voting by a show of hands, shouting people down, pairing with individuals who, at least superficially, seem to favour the resolution of the meeting (usually the competitor for power) even though this pairing may well be abused before the final decision. In one example the democratic leader paired with the competitor and they were about to make a decision that totally ignored the views of all other group members. Just before the decision was taken, the competitor, who until then had encouraged the leader to take a strong line according to his own views, suddenly denounced him as a poor leader who was riding roughshod over the group. He appealed to the group to follow his lead and the meeting ended in chaos. Some typical patterns are commonly seen in the exercise. Leaders will try to be democratic at the outset and for some considerable time will often try to resist the 'market forces' in the group. However, even voting techniques based on a show of hands can be interfered with by the group, and the leader will often pair with anyone who will agree with his or her views and the need to form a coalition. Decisions may be made by leaders if they feel that only one person agrees with them, even if this were the cynic or the clown! This pairing in turn makes the leader vulnerable to further disruptive shaping of their behaviour by the partner if the latter needed to reach any sort of decision. Other leader-volunteers have tried to further open up or even change the topic of the discussion in order to achieve a feeling of reassurance that the group is capable of making any sort of decision at all. The effect of this play is in fact to provide the group with an additional opportunity to compound the confusion being generated. Another common group outcome influenced by a harassed leader is the lowering of group goals, from the level of decision making to that of open discussion.

After the role-plays, participants are given feedback about both their behaviour and the processes generated in the group. A video recording enables a more accurate assessment of group behaviour, including the examination of the effects of non-verbal communication. Discussion groups and workshops can follow up the issues raised in the role-play and their relevance to the way in which real-life staff meetings are conducted. Although the conditions outlined in this exercise are extreme, the conditions for the predicted shifts in leadership style are present; that is, the dominance of personal agendas amongst team members, an emphasis on group goals, and an ambiguity about the processes and skills necessary for effective goal attainment (i.e. lack of time boundaries and instruction on consensus-seeking behaviours). Less extreme variation in the manipulation of these conditions still gives rise to similar patterns of group behaviour and an important point can be made here about the responsibility of group behaviour as well as individual characteristics being a vital determinant of leadership styles. Other exercises in this series deal with the maintenance of more effective group and team behaviours and roles.

Exercise two

Another exercise on role behaviour in groups offers an opportunity to experience the processes by which groups can force individuals to adopt specific role behaviours (stereotyping). In this exercise a group convenes either to discuss a topic of importance in residential care or to role-play a specific organizational meeting. Participants wear caps on which are written role descriptions and, if necessary, behavioural instructions about how other members of the group should respond. Thus, each member knows the (potential) role of everyone but him- or herself. The group is instructed to operate in such a way that they respond to each person as if they had the personal characteristics implied by the role title, some of which can include cynic, font of wisdom, intellectualizer, practical or reality-oriented, clown, old hand, naive or inexperienced, a sensitive supporter of others, leader, the silent member, or the too talkative person (subtitled 'ignore me'). This exercise can provide a powerful demonstration of some more of the generally less visible behaviour in groups. Participants frequently report the difficulty they experience in resisting behavioural changes that are being forced upon them by the actions and attitudes of others. The effects are even more dramatic when team members are given roles that conflict with their observed, normal behaviour. For example, even the most insensitive individual can be encouraged to behave in a thoughtful and sensitive manner towards others if he or she receives messages that he or she is capable of doing this. Knowledge, or lack of it, about the exact nature of the ascribed role (people often guess the role they have been assigned by the end of the exercise) seems to have little effect on the emotional effect of the behavioural changes wrought by group pressure, although it will obviously prompt an individual to look within themselves for appropriate role behaviour they can bring to the exercise. In this sense, the exercise can also prompt the rehearsal or acquisition of more effective social group behaviours by assigning roles thought to be valuable to positive group processes. Of course, the exercise does primarily serve to highlight how group pressures can affect roles. In one example, a participant wore a cap with no role behaviour on it whatsoever. During the course of the exercise she was ascribed qualities of extreme virtue and intellect and also denigrated for her lack of social awareness and adjustment. Other participants later related feeling threatened and uncomfortable in the presence of this unknown quantity, and the person occupying the role felt at once both powerful and impotent as a result of the obvious confusion her presence was creating in the group. This later developed into a deep discussion on the impact of new members in the team. Menninger Foundation Staff (1971) point to this as a potent factor in the disorganization of team functioning. Once again, feedback about group and individual behaviours, including videotaping, and theoretical input about group processes enable this exercise to make a valuable contribution to the team's awareness of the problems, pitfalls and, most importantly, the advantages of co-operative working.

EMPATHIC SKILLS

The capacity to appreciate the way in which another views the world and relates to it is seen as a vital element in therapeutic skills (Rogers 1951; Truax and Carkhuff 1967), and is a component of normal interpersonal relationships. Empathic skills can help staff in the process of learning to rely on their colleagues and to be able to predict how someone is going to behave or think in a given situation. These skills can be facilitated by a continuing process of close contact and communication, and the mutual, respectful sharing of views of common issues. Specific exercises can augment this process where necessary.

The pioneering work of Moreno (1936) in the field of psychodrama has provided some useful techniques for developing empathic skills, which are now incorporated into a range of human relations exercises. Role-reversal techniques (Blattner 1975), where participants each adopt the role of the other in a replay of an interaction, can help individuals see a situation from the standpoint of another person and can be a useful technique in the resolution of interpersonal conflict. A variety of 'doubling' techniques have been developed by psychodramatists. These involve one person speaking for another person in an interaction (Blattner 1975) and can facilitate the skill of predicting the emotional, intellectual, or behavioural reactions of another. In the role-play of a discussion for example, one person can stand behind a participant and answer on his or her behalf. A process of 'checking out' with the silent participant enables the 'double' to refine and sharpen their capacity to understand the standpoint of another. The technique can also be used to help people become more honest, open, and less definitive by following a participant's answer with comments that the 'double' feels the 'doubled' person really wishes to express and which may be considerably discrepant with what is actually said. Used in a role-play of staff meetings, for example, this technique can facilitate the disclosure of hidden agendas. Another technique to develop empathic skills demands that, first, participants list four qualities about themselves that they like and four qualities that they feel uncomfortable with (Blattner 1975). These self-descriptions are exchanged with a chosen partner who attempts to articulate how it would feel to own those qualities. Each response can be checked against the other person's views for accuracy and the development of a closer, mutual understanding. The view that a person holds about the world (the constant system (Kelly 1955) or representational models (Bandler and Grinder 1976) that have been developed to predict and understand the world) is built upon experiences that can reach far back into an individual's life. Asking team members to describe a positive and a negative work experience with a series of adjectives that seem most appropriate and significant, and following this with a request for individuals to spend some time thinking about the significance of the words and what they reflect about life-style, can be another technique for helping individuals to a better understanding of colleagues in the work situation. One participant described a positive experience with terms like 'strength' and 'security'. It turned out that in each of her most rewarding work moments she had been on duty with a particular senior member of staff who represented some of the stability she had missed because of an absent father. This disclosure enabled her to feel free to ask for support and advice when necessary from a wider range of colleagues, who also became more aware of the specific circumstances in the residential setting when the individual needed support that she had previously been unable to ask for.

Further exploration in empathic skills can be undertaken in a 'group phantasy' (Schutz 1967; Lewis and Streatfield 1970). A group is asked to relax, close their eyes, and imagine themselves to be participating in a social scene described by the facilitator, or by one of the group in a prior discussion. The situation could be one describing a work situation. One person is then asked to describe people in his or her own phantasy, imagining him- or herself to be one of the actors. Other group members then identify with the speaker and express how they would feel in the situation being described. Frank (1978) found that phantasy-related training methods did facilitate performance on tests of intuitive perceptual judgements. This adds some strength to the long-held clinical belief that a therapist's willingness to permit his or her private thought processes to develop in response to client material and a willingness to attend to the meaning of these processes, lead to improved intuitive awareness of the patient's situation. It is normal that intuitive observations, impressions, and judgements only receive conscious articulation at a relatively late stage in the diagnostic process and such techniques may draw staff attention to the need for pooling and making realistic clinical sense of their own emotional and cognitive reactions both at the level of refining high levels of empathic skills and prompting a specific focus of attention onto clinical judgement behaviour.

CONFLICT NEGOTIATION

Throughout the training programme, looking at intra-team tensions that can reduce the effectiveness of the team in achieving its primary task, it will be necessary through discussion or role-play, or both, to prompt awareness of effective negotiation skills for dealing with interpersonal conflict. The topics of such conflict can be myriad, ranging from disagreement over behaviour management issues to tension arising from a feeling of not being able to confront a colleague about lack of support during a crisis, mismanagement of a difficult scene with residents, or unreliability at work. Stepsis (1974) argues for a distinction between conflicts over value judgements that can be very difficult to reach a compromise over, as opposed to real or tangible conflict. Provided that the training programme has created a sufficient improvement in interpersonal relationships through the use of discussion, consensus-seeking exercises, trust games (Schutz 1967; Lewis and Streatfield 1970; Brandon and Phillips 1977), and the use of effective skills in communication and the giving of feedback, then the skills of successful negotiation can be introduced wherever conflict is not being resolved. It should be noted that as with all exercises, the level of input from the facilitator must take into account the current strength of the group in the interpersonal areas being examined. Skills of negotiation include the ability to diagnose the nature of the problem, effectiveness in initiating negotiation in a manner that will not further increase tension, skill at listening to other points of view and attempting to hear what is being said and meant, and the use of problem-solving processes, such as brainstorming, all of which can generate a sufficient range of alternative solutions (Stepsis 1974).

As an initial stage in the development of these skills, participants can be asked to recall the details of an interpersonal conflict that has not been resolved. They are asked to relax and imagine themselves in a situation where they meet their 'antagonist' in circumstances that indicate that painful issues are not far below the surface. The group, as individuals, are asked to imagine how their 'phantasy' develops naturally. Do they avoid the confrontation altogether (e.g. by leaving the room), do they diffuse the feeling (e.g. by becoming angry with the other person over generalized issues, but not the matter in hand), or do they confront situations effectively and clearly, and non-vindictively attempt to pinpoint the issue? Group discussions on the various personal styles for handling such conflicts can follow, using role-play techniques to demonstrate both appropriate and inappropriate behaviour. If it has not already moved that way, the developing discussion can be geared to introducing specific team-related conflict, in order to ensure, as in all team-building exercises, that the focus of training must always return to work-oriented themes.

SUMMARY

In Chapters 4, 5, and 6 we have examined issues geared to training staff in team skills. We have stressed the importance of such an approach for the success of residential care practice without such techniques leading to the development of a staff-oriented culture that overlooks the needs of children. All anxieties must come back to drawing parallels with real work situations, perhaps through role-play. Each exercise, and we have listed only a few, can generate a tremendous amount of material that can be developed and used as an indicator of further training needs both at context and contact levels. For example, the experience of the 'good group member' in the role-plays we have described can lead to valuable discussion and educational input on role functions in groups, from the task function of seeking and giving information and opinion, co-ordinating and evaluating ideas, to the maintenance functions of encouraging less assertive staff to talk, seeking consensus, giving and receiving feedback, setting standards, and processing group information. In one exercise the 'good member' found it impossible to intervene in such a disruptive group and fell silent, becoming the butt of displaced feelings from other dysfunctional members of the group who saw him as opting out, even ill. The leaders of such exercises will need to be flexible in their approach as the natural skills and tensions of the team will often make it necessary to re-arrange the order of activities – to bring some forward, to delete others – in order to meet the specific needs of the group and its individual members.

Team work and compatibility are important components of residential care; the skills of team members need to be recognized and co-ordinated, and, above all, valued. Developing skills in working together, involving an appreciation of roles and behaviours that impede or improve team effectiveness, is vital if the team is to achieve its primary tasks of care and treatment, containing anxiety, and making sense of feelings evoked in staff by the client group. Training intact work teams provides an opportunity to develop lasting improvements in the quality of team processes and the real pattern of relationships that must be coped with if they are to be enjoyed as sources of support and satisfaction. More experience of this type of training input is needed in order to refine its value for organizations.

7 Personal and Therapeutic Relationships

Most residential workers and clinicians would agree that the nature of their relationship with their clients is of paramount importance. In spite of some understandable criticisms of the unthinking use of the term 'relationship' as a coverall for most therapeutic activities that enables them to be acknowledged but not properly and operationally described (Hoghugi 1978), there is a body of literature that can substantially clarify this most important element of human behaviour, that is, after all, held in high regard by most normal people. As it is within the context of interpersonal relationships that the important activities of counselling and supervision occur, these will be considered as a unit of discussion.

Knopka (1955 : 679) talked of 'a significant and helpful relationship between the houseparent or counsellor and each individual child'. By meaningful relationship Knopka meant a 'warm and sensitive relationship with deep respect for the personality of each child'. This is a definition that for all its human appeal does lack some operational definition and lends itself to Hoghugi's criticism of the term (and activity of) relationship as 'social work's sacred cow' (Hoghugi 1978 : 145) that should not really be emphasized as either indicative of a treatment goal or as a valid therapeutic intervention. However, the literature and thinking on residential care abounds with the use of the term, both as a therapeutic tool (Aichorn 1944) and as a goal in its own right. Many studies on the criteria for admission to residential care see deficits in relationship capacity as clear referral patterns (Aichorn 1944; Easson 1969; Moordock 1979). However inexact these criteria may be in their usage, there is no doubt that the prevalence of thinking about interpersonal relationships demands that an examination of the issue be a valid theme for staff development programmes. Even Hoghugi (1978) effectively concedes this point by saying that as positive relationships may be considered as beneficial to the processes of care treatment and behaviour management, so may poor relationships .make these tasks less pleasant and more difficult. If this is so, then we have a duty to ensure that children in care receive the type of attention and intervention that will best aid their progress back into the community.

There are three major justifications for examining the role of relationships in residential care:

(1) Every child in care has a right to something approaching the level of nurturance and affection that is afforded to all adolescents. As Davies (1976) points out, child-care practice must encompass the giving and receiving of love and affection, and acknowledge the reality of acknowledging the 'parallel emotions in both the cared for and the care giver'. Formal treatment processes, if too 'programmed', may effectively put an emotional distance between staff and young people (Watkins 1979) by attributing responsibility for caring behaviour and its consequence to the dictates of a system rather than to the actions of people. Residential environments can thus become 'bland, inocuous . . . steeped in expertise . . . strictly controlled . . . passing for worthwhile experience' (Davies 1976 : 28).

(2) If definite deficits in the capacity to make and maintain interpersonal relationships can be properly established as part of a direct referral picture, then relationships with staff, if used properly and thoughtfully, can be a valid forum for the development and maintenance of appropriate levels of skills and personal qualities.

(3) Once the inevitable relationships that are bound to develop within such an intense living environment as a residential unit have been formed and have for individual children been invested with a certain degree of significance, then those relationships can operate as a source of praise and approval for the development and maintenance of a whole range of

desired changes in behaviour and attitudes (Krasner 1961).

The manner in which children naturally conduct their relationships with residential staff may also provide valuable clues to the nature and influence of the interpersonal relationships they have previously experienced and the manner in which social interactions have (and, indeed, still may be) influencing and shaping their behaviour. Therefore, the use of relationships in residential care practice can help a more thorough-going behavioural and clinical assessment of the particular difficulties of young clients and, as Alderton points out (1965), opportunities to help young people change, if necessary, their expectations of and behaviour towards significant people by presenting a consistent pattern of staff response to child demands that does not confirm previously held beliefs about adults.

If relationships between residential staff and disturbed young people are capable of putting people at risk (Hoghugi 1979), and if it is inevitable, as it is, that interpersonal relationships, whether based solely on mutual liking, perceptions, and interests or on a more intense level, will occur, then all residential staff have a deep-rooted responsibility to ensure that the quality of relationships they provide is both genuine and therapeutically useful.

Some writers have attempted to clarify the structural elements of therapeutic relationships (see Alderton 1965; Adler 1971; Schapiro and Tyrka 1975; Bancroft 1979). Bancroft sees that the therapist can facilitate the treatment process by suggesting new ideas about and coping in problem areas, giving instructive feedback, and undertaking a range of activities that depend on the degree of mutual input and liking between client and therapist. These include increasing the client's understanding of why he or she has difficulty in coping in certain ways by in turn becoming familiarized with the characteristics of the client's social environment; by confronting the client with reality; by disclosing something of his or her own personal values; by helping a client to express feelings; by facilitating interpersonal communication both between client and therapist and client and significant others, for example parents, whose relationships may serve to shape and influence problem behaviour; by getting the client to commit him- or herself to change; and by fostering independence and discouraging dependence. The therapist should become an available resource to be used by the client rather than being someone who 'takes over' in a therapeutic relationship.

These elements are present in other models of therapeutic relationships. The presentation of reality to the client in a non-judgemental fashion, to disclose those aspects of oneself (as a therapist) that may be useful in facilitating the learning process, through a process of modelling, the task of helping a client to make sense of the connections between their experiences; to become grounded in reality and explore the potential advantages of new relationships, new experiences, and new behaviours are part of Schapiro's and Tyrka's (1975) analysis of the helping relationship. This also focuses on the interpersonal, feeling, elements of the relationship more than does Bancroft's (1979). The therapist's main task is to repair trust by providing a relationship in which it is safe to be open, to experience feelings, and to risk anxiety, rejection, conflict, and loss. This process of being able to experience unpleasant feelings from a position of safety is analagous to the behavioural technique of desensitiza-tion (Wolpé 1969) and is described as such, in behavioural terms, by Sulzer (1962) who sees psychotherapy as primarily a learning process that in many ways can be restated in behavioural terms. One of the most significant aspects of Schapiro's and Tyrka's (1975) model is that it sees the therapist (or counsellor) as someone upon whom the client depends to gather together all the fragments of information about his or her life in order 'to hold them securely', to be able to invest meaning and cohesion into this maze of experience so that some control over life processes can be achieved and change brought about. An independent comment from a residential worker reflected this point: 'Peter talks to a lot of staff informally, testing out their views on a range of issues from behaviour and values, their consequences etc., and he tells me of all that is said. Once a week or so he comes back to me and clearly expects me to be making sense of this on his behalf.' Clearly there are times and situations when Bancroft's notion of fostering independence may have to bend slightly to allow young people who lack the emotional or intellectual resources to do the thinking for themselves, to be reliant on significant people for specific tasks.

Carl Rogers (1951) has spelt out the necessary conditions of the therapeutic relationship that will enable 'client change'. Good interpersonal communication, and a capacity to empathize with and be able to both experience and transmit unconditional positive regard for the client are, for Rogers, vital elements of the therapeutic contact. By showing empathy (or understanding), respect (or caring), and concreteness (being specific), the therapist can help clients along the road to self-exploration and understanding, and the client can be helped to act on this improved understanding if he or she receives from the therapist feelings of genuineness, confrontation (i.e. the presentation of reality), and immediacy (i.e. dealing with the here-and-now). These aspects of therapist qualities encourage the client to try out new ways of behaving and thinking in communicating in the comparative safety of a counselling relationship (Rogers 1951). Moustakas (1959 : 111) has argued that the relationship is both the means and an end to therapeutic change; it is the essential dimension in child therapy and perhaps 'the only significant one'.

Whilst it can be relatively simple to describe the structural components of a therapeutic relationship, the means whereby the relationship is established and maintained demands some more thought and care. Schapiro (1975), in reviewing the outcome of research into psychotherapeutic processes, claims promising results have been made with 'relationship therapy'. In reviewing Parson's (1966) study of group therapy, which involved establishing a therapeutic sequence consisting of a supportive relationship, providing interpretation and differential reinforcement, reducing stress surrounding and associated with antisocial behaviour, followed by discussion of a return to the community, Schapiro concluded that the therapist seemed to gain influence over the clients and then used this influence in the process of achieving personal change. The therapist's significance can be used to strengthen new ways of coping. This view is similar to Klein's (1973) notion of the 'indispensibility' of the therapist for the client, and is reflected also in Brendtro's (1969 in Adler 1971) definition of interpersonal relationships as they occur in residential care. Establishing a relationship with an emotionally disturbed or maladjusted child consists of three components: increasing the child's communicativeness with the adult; helping the child respond more to the help and care offered by adults; and increasing the tendency of the child to model appropriate behaviour demonstrated by the adult.

Two crucial points emerge from this discussion. First, in most models of therapeutic relationships an important element acknowledged by most writers is the provision of a safe, anxiety-free environment or psychological space in which a client can experience behaviours, thoughts, or feelings previously associated with painful, unpleasant, or even disastrous consequences. This relief of anxiety in the presence of a responsive skilled adult is likely to increase the social power of the therapist through a process of simple association (i.e. his or her presence – the relationship – is associated with relief from, or reduction in, anxiety that previously may have been experienced as overwhelming). This process is analagous to the behavioural technique of desensitization (Sulzer 1962; Wolpé 1969), and seems to provide the means whereby the therapist has the significance or the 'social reinforcement value' to be able to encourage behaviour change, and, more importantly, an exploration of the young person's inner world. Virginia Axline (1947) has clarified some of the techniques that can also be useful in helping a therapist or caring adult achieve, in the eyes of the child client, a degree of significance that allows the child to value the therapist or counsellor as someone who can help resolve issues and emotional problems (i.e. relieve anxiety).

Second, the conscious development of a positive relationship with a child will involve the use of good interpersonal skills such as providing social approval and other rewarding experiences. In the residential setting, where often the young people have had many painful experiences in their relationships with adults, this will mean the provision of leisure and other experiences that will allow the child to enjoy the residential experience. The child should be accepted for what he or she is. This concept sometimes causes concern as it appears to imply that there will be no boundaries on a child's deviant or acting-out behaviour. Indeed, Aichorn's (1944) original model allowed for this: he claimed that by allowing young people to act out their inner anxieties and delinquent behaviour, this eventually made them realize that there were no limits being set: the young people exhibited panic reactions and then a pattern of socially acceptable behaviour. It is difficult to see how this could have been achieved without some limit setting or instruction, whether overt or covert, about the nature of desired behaviour change. There is now quite strong evidence that therapists of different theoretical orientations can produce in clients patterns of 'classic' symptoms that match their own working assumptions through a covert, often unintentional and unconscious, shaping of clients' verbal and active behaviour by subtle forms of social reinforcement during therapeutic interviews (Greenspoon 1962; Sulzer 1967). Reflective listening skills (i.e. responding verbally to a child's expressions of feelings and behaviour without adding one's own perceptions or feelings to the response) can be taught or used in conjunction with limit setting (i.e. setting behavioural boundaries) and structuring a caring environment in order to allow young people to take more responsibility for their behaviour and improve their relationship with significant adults (Grisberg *et al.* 1978). Permissiveness in Axline's (1947) model allows the child to express his or her feelings freely, and, presumably, without the fear of unpleasant consequences being realized. In this way, verbal skills are being strengthened along with the process of labelling and identifying feeling states. By having these feelings reflected back the child may gain insight into his or her behaviour and hence learn to take some responsibility for making choices about problems that confront him or her. Axline also reinforces the view that the counsellor should assist or follow, rather than direct, the child in the learning process. It is a gradual rather than a sudden process, and, in common with other relationship models, some limits are essential so that counselling and its style and content are related to real values and so that the young person recognizes the responsibility he or she must take in the therapeutic process.

Relationships in residental care are often characterized by a counselling or helping/enabling element. That is, staff use the significance they have achieved in order to help a youngster make sense of, and try to resolve, some of the problems that stop him or her from living a satisfied existence. Counselling within relationships can, therefore, serve a number of functions. It can develop an adequate picture of the child's world as he or she sees it; establish the significance and meaning of events and interrelationships in that world; and help and enable the young person to develop effective problem-solving skills based on a clearer understanding of the nature of his or her difficulties and the blocks to treatment or change that the child erects. Whilst the appropriate goal is for staff to modify the behaviour of young people, the reverse can occur. That is, the behaviour and feelings of staff can, in turn, be shaped and influenced by client behaviour (Lichtenburg and Hummel 1976). Young people entering the care situation bring with them more or less well-formed attitudes and expectations about adult roles and behaviour based on experience with parents, child-care staff, and other significant individuals whose influence and interaction may not have been appropriate of fitting. Young people cannot easily rid themselves of the anxiety-laden memories that have guided their interpersonal relationships. They will test out potential new relationships to the limit, thus often forcing staff into taking on some of the attributes and behaviour of others who have hurt or rejected the child. It is important that staff do not confirm young people's distorted expectations of them by behaving inappropriately (Alderton 1965; Adler 1971). Treatment may falter or fail if children succeed in evoking from staff, in a manner that cannot be monitored or controlled, responses that the child has experienced in the past that have been in their own right destructive. Staff must be aware that residential care provides a challenge to young people in the sense of offering alternative models for behaving and coping. In the process of adjustment, anxiety, fear, and acting out can be expected as the child is forced to modify some of his or her core concepts about him- or herself and others (Kelly 1955). In other words, the child will seek active confirmation about his or her beliefs and views about his or her world and the people in it. Only by knowing the frame of reference that guides a young person's behaviour can staff seek ways to act that will fail to confirm the beliefs we wish to change (and the behaviour that is consequent on those beliefs). It is clear from observations of the perceptions of child-care workers about their own tasks (Holtby 1972) that most staff see counselling and interpersonal relationships as vehicles for personal growth and the shaping of more effective behaviour, starting from the point of trying to understand what the child is saying about him- or herself. Personality development is highly dependent upon significant and appropriate communication exchanges in the areas of personal identity, relationships, co-operation, feeling, interpersonal feelings, thinking, interpersonal thinking, intra- and interpersonal expectations, and values (Reutsch 1972). Parent-child communication, according to Reutsch, can become a pathological process if adult responses are either over- or underdiscriminative, are one-sided (relevant only to specific situations), or interfere with the correction of information so that young people adopt or develop either a distorted or misinformed world-view. The selective reinforcement of the expression of particular attitudes, feelings, and behaviours, and the related speech and behaviour patterns, lead to the formation of thinking patterns that in turn can shape and influence the perception of future events and consequent personal reactions to these events. The course of both effective and disturbed communication is shaped by the content and form of feedback from parents and significant others. Through such a process, Reutsch (1972) claims, distorted interpersonal communication can 'prejudice the outcome of an exchange'. If only irritating or disruptive behaviours are responded to by parents, children may come to learn that inappropriate behaviours signify the initiation of significant communication exchanges, for example, eliciting care or attention from significant others.

Residential staff must try to avoid being drawn into the

distorted linguistic, perceptual, and behavioural world of the child whilst at the same time being able to appreciate it and provide a richer and more balanced interpersonal experience that will begin to modify and enrich the perceptions of young people. The way in which young people talk about their problems, experiences, and self-image may well reflect how their thought and behaviour patterns have been previously shaped and reinforced. In resisting and altering the direction of these processes, staff have to provide alternative models for behaviour and thinking (Bandura and Walters 1963) that can draw on all aspects and experiences of the residential day (Polsky 1963; Bettelheim and Wright 1972). All aspects of a child's development and activity must be considered valuable areas for potential change. The (mere) presentation of self, by staff, in a consistent and genuine manner will offer the adolescent possibly the first opportunity to have his or her beliefs, views, and behaviours challenged. If this process is to be maximized, then it must become an essentially interactive one that can beneficially draw, among other things, on some of the established principles of counselling.

COUNSELLING

In common with other significant developments in the area of counselling and behaviour change (Miechenbaum and Goodman 1971), Lembo (1976) identifies the need to discover the irrational beliefs that govern or determine perception and action. With young people who are taciturn, resentful, fearful, inarticulate, or extremely anxious, evidence of these irrational beliefs must be culled from a wide range of observations and inferences in the residential environment, and regularly cross-checked and shared, both with colleagues and young people where possible. The very act of talking about significant issues with disturbed adolescents may well reactivate and reinforce the belief that adults are dangerous and working against the protection of the child, and may thus evoke resistances that prevent further investigation. Residential staff must, therefore, develop techniques for understanding the world of the adolescent and for motivating him or her towards a commitment to change that does not seem to threaten his or her existence.

Counselling practice guidelines developed elsewhere in the helping professions can demonstrate, by comparison, the degree of professionalism that is demanded and often seen as an ongoing part of residential practice. Effective counselling is based on four basic assumptions: (1) resolving problems is most likely to occur when current methods of coping with reality are focused on, and when young people can trust, take risks, and take full responsibility for personal thoughts and feelings. (2) Self-defeating behaviours are most likely to be removed or replaced when young people can be encouraged to participate in behaviour and activities that are incompatible with the problem. (3) Expected or desired treatment outcomes are more likely when instruction, appropriate models, and (4) continuous practices are built into the counselling and helping process (Lembo 1976). The residential care model that utilizes all aspects of a young person's daily experiences for potential therapeutic movement (Redl and Wineman 1952; Polsky and Claster 1968; Whittaker and Treichman 1972; Bettleheim and Wright 1972) involves more complexity than in this model as it has, first and foremost, to create and provide conditions that are essential for the counselling process (i.e. a climate of trust and safety, a presentation of (adult) self that allows the significance of staff to young people to be more realistic and fulfilling than their previous experiences so that the 'modelling' task can be implemented (Wotherspoon 1972)).

Counsellor eclecticism (Keat 1974; Lembo 1976) (i.e. taking the best aspects of various theoretical and practice models and integrating them into a unified approach) can also enhance counsellor effectiveness especially if they can demonstrate what may be called 'effective helping skills' (Danish and Hauer 1977). That is, listening intently to the young person's experiences, ideas, and feelings, assessing clients unconditionally; assessing ideas, feelings, and behaviour; gathering reliable information about problems related to personal circumstances; asking clients to commit themselves to change and take full responsibility for their behaviour (a notion similar to that of Bancroft (1979) but one that is the cornerstone of residential care success, difficult as it is to achieve); establishing realistic treatment goals; helping young people to replace self-defeating behaviours and thought processes ('magical thinking' Bandler and Grinder 1976) by more realistic and appropriate coping methods and by helping young people to use realistic self-help strategies, develop problem-solving skills and interpersonal relationships.

In residential care, most, if not all, of these activities are woven into the continuous daily fabric of institutional life where staff can develop the capacity to be sensitive to the ongoing ability of young people to become involved in such activities, especially those relating to commitment and trust. Deviant patterns of behaviour may provide the only personal significant reinforcements that the young person has in terms of self-esteem, relationships, status, and identity, and they will often be reluctant to yield such behaviours without some form of depressive reaction (Rinsley 1971) until or unless they have safely experienced viable alternatives that accord with their value systems and are also visibly a source of more effective social, survival, remedial, and compensatory activities (Maier 1971) that provide appropriate interpersonal skills. The internalization of controls (Rotter 1975; Altmaier *et al.* 1979) and adequate levels of verbal and cognitive skills are prerequisites of this counselling approach for young people with a wide range of crippling emotional, educational, social, and behavioural deficits.

COUNSELLING SKILLS

Appropriate training in counselling skills demands first of all a clear definition of effective counselling behaviour, and a number of studies have spelt out details of both counselling skills and other factors that affect the effectiveness of counselling as a treatment approach. Boyd and Roach (1977) identified interpersonal communication skills that led to more effective counselling of relationship difficulties. These included actively listening and receiving messages (i.e. listening to what is meant as well as what is being said); and sending clear, direct messages and verbal expressions of respect or esteem towards others. These skills, when possessed by counsellors and taught to clients, both through instructional and modelling methods, led to significant improvements in problematic relationships. Other research studies (see Bergland and Quatrano 1976; Spooner and Stone 1977) have isolated skills that are basic to the maintenance of effective counselling:

(1) *Goal setting*. Included in this skill is an understanding of what the client feels he or she is capable of achieving, through an analysis of what he or she says, in terms of altered behaviours or altered circumstances. It also includes exploration of alternative ways to handle problem-solving and self-help issues.

(2) *Confrontation*. The counsellor calls the client's attention to behaviours of which he or she may be unaware, and makes statements that challenge the client and point out discrepancies between his or her actions and verbally expressed ideas. The counsellor may also make statements that offer a new perspective to presenting problems.

(3) *Reflection statement* involves rephrasing the content or the feeling of what the client is saying about him- or herself.

(4) *Interpretation summary* entails pulling together the strands of meaning from all that the client is saying.

(3) and (4) as skills combined together reflect Schapiro's (1975) definition of the therapeutic task which says that a therapist holds all a patient's verbalizations on his or her behalf, synthesizes and integrates them, makes sense of them for the client, and makes the therapist significant *for* the client.

(5) *Structuring statements* include the description of the counselling process, planning limits and boundaries, giving reassurance, and establishing 'rapport'.

(6) *Probing*. This refers to any questions that gives the counsellor insight into the client's problems, or that clarifies understanding.

(7) *Mutual verbal responses*. Verbal or non-verbal messages

that signal the counsellors continuing interest.

(8) *Self-disclosure* involves identifying elements of one's own behaviour if it can aid the modelling of appropriate coping strategies.

(9) *Information giving*. This means giving practical help and advice.

During training sessions for counsellors it was found that trainees felt that the skills of reflection, probing, confrontation, and rapport were the most useful counselling tools, and formed, along with interpretative and summarizing skills, the major proportion of observed counselling behaviours. Bergland and Quatrano, Spooner and Stone (1977), noted that probing (i.e. asking questions) was a favourite intervention in the counselling process as observed during training sessions but that without checking it could turn a counselling session into an interrogation.

Other studies have shown that skills in the communication of verbal and non-verbal messages to the client are vital to an effective counselling process. Clients attached to therapists who sent out verbal messages that were inconsistent with non-verbal ones (e.g. body posture, eye contact, and leg positioning) perceived the counsellor as less genuine and more emotionally distant. These perceptions were strengthened if the verbal responses were positive and the non-verbal ones negative. Such inconsistent messages are often seen as deceitful and dishonest, and only the congruence of both verbal and non-verbal messages will convey genuineness, and reduce interpersonal distance (Graves and Robinson 1966; Cottle 1976).

Counselling effectiveness is also directly related to the social interests of counsellors (Zanski *et al*. 1977). A clear relationship has been demonstrated between sucessful counselling outcome and levels of warmth, empathy, and genuineness (Rogers 1951; Truax and Carkhuff 1967). Differences between counsellors, in terms of the quality of their work, may be more useful than theoretical orientation and specific method types in explaining outcome (Keat 1974; Leventhal and Slemburg 1977; and Zanski 1977). Empathy has been found to be related to self-confidence and levels of social interest (Ansbacher 1968 and Lin 1973), and it appears that the personal qualities of counsellors are a pervasive and more promising prediction of counsellors' effectiveness than is reference to the theoretical persuasion of the counsellor. Social interest has been defined by reference both to individual behaviour (along dimensions of gregarious versus tendency to withdraw; activity–passivity; benevolent–aggressive; befriended–mistreated) and to the individual (counsellor's) perception of his or her environment as friendly, nurturing or threatening, frustrating, accepting or rejecting, or capable of promoting self-esteem and independence. Counsellor levels of social interest were found to be significantly correlated with levels of client satisfaction in the counselling process, self-acceptance, and sociability (i.e. counsellors can facilitate the development of like social behaviours in clients through modelling and social reinforcement techniques).

This finding is particularly important for residential practice: it reinforces the importance of the widely held view that residential staff should be appointed not only for professional expertise but also for personal characteristics that have in themselves two important functions: they widen the young person's perception of the real world and potentially provide more opportunities for growth, and they also contribute towards a climate of informality and safety that is crucial to effective counselling. This finding also establishes a firmer relationship between these qualities and the professional task of counselling, thus indicating the importance of training to facilitate the best use of these skills.

In a residential environment the treatment emphasis has to provide a balance between meeting group and individual needs (Polsky and Claster 1968) where the social culture is strengthened by improving the relevance and depth of interpersonal communication amongst both staff and young people. The use that residential staff make of the counselling process enables them to exploit all relevant living experiences to further the resolution of conflicts and the problem-solving capacity of the client group. For Diggles (1970), the goal of residential treatment is 'ego-adequacy', whereby young people learn, through the acceptance of tasks and relationships, to control and modify their behaviour in order to achieve stable levels of appropriate behaviours, strengthened by positive reinforcements that derive from a 'meaningful inter-action with his environment'. Reality testing is the natural consequence of the continual experience of attempting new behaviours in a natural setting and internalizing their consequences. These successful interactions with the environment lead to effective learning about reality and improve the capacity of the young person to integrate his or her experiences (Dymond and Donnelly 1969). The emotionally disturbed and deprived child has a more limited capacity to understand and react appropriately to the demands of his or her environment and he or she is therefore more dependent upon the system and above all the staff to provide information, control, behaviour management, socializing skills, and the enhancement of his or her relatively poor repertoire of communication skills. In Diggles's model, staff are around to provide signs and cues about behaviour, and, as counsellors, help to draw together internal and external experiences, and to act in a directive fashion that enables youngsters to experience reality successfully, to teach them a repertoire of appropriate social and problem-solving behaviours, to appreciate the range and limitations of problem-solving resources in their environment, and to facilitate the internalization of values and controls. The child-care counsellor is there to try to achieve a 'fit' between the internal and often chaotic inner world of the child with the more stable external reality; to help the child to gain or regain control over his or her behaviour. The use of relationships and counselling skills is a vital complementary activity to behavioural management programmes, allowing for effective strengthening of internal controls through the development of cognitive and verbal skills and controls, and the improvement of the child's capacity to understand, label, and control his or her own feelings. Hill and Gormally (1977) found that probing (questioning) behaviours on the part of counsellors resulted in more discussion of feelings, as their function was to stimulate appropriate client responses. This process can help staff to discover what sort of 'self-statements' young people make about themselves, their behaviour and its significance and meaning for them (Keat 1974; Highlen and Voight 1978). Schwartz (1976) found that a major contribution to some behaviourial deficits (e.g. non-assertive behaviour) was related to the nature of the individual's 'internal dialogue'. The recent interest in treatment strategies based on cognitive restructuring techniques that help a client to think differently about themselves or their problems has shown that in some areas the modification of the client's thinking patterns was superior to programmes geared to modifying tangible behaviours in the treatment of certain adolescent problems (Glass *et al*. 1976 : 520–26). However, such differential results rely on the adequate diagnosis of client problems as resulting from either a lack in behaviour skills or from other factors such as self-perceived anxiety, negative self-perceptions, or expectations about the outcome (consequence) of behaviour (Rotter 1975). Some children do not demonstrate appropriate coping behaviours because they are afraid, for whatever reason, of the consequences.

Residential staff also need to be aware that as adolescents move from late childhood dramatic changes can occur in the way in which they think and process information (Dooley *et al*. 1978). Younger children tend to see events as resulting from their own actions whilst adolescents begin to understand the relationship of cause and effect in their environment more fully, and begin to understand and conceptualize their own behaviour. Giving directive advice can be seen as distancing and over-controlling in adult-to-adult therapeutic situations, whereas it has been clearly established that young children and adolescents see advice-giving as a signal of involvement and caring (Dooley *et al*. 1978). Developmental stages of problem-solving can be identified with younger or more immature, defensive, or inarticulate adolescents, who prefer direct problem-solving techniques to those based on reflectiveness, self-examination, and disclosure, which come with greater experience of coping with the problems of living.

Decreases in the level of self-disclosure in young people may reflect defensiveness in the face of a confronting style of counselling but may also reflect a more normal adolescent concern with how they present themselves to the world and others that marks a new move towards an independence from adults (Dooley *et al.* 1978). Young people in care often worry or panic that talking about their personal problems may either break up the family, lead to rejection from others, or lead to the development of treatment strategies that night mean longer periods in care (Zarie and Boyd 1977). The personal, subjective expectations that people have about the consequences of behaviour are highly significant determinants of observed behaviour (Rotter 1954, 1975; Norwicki and Duke 1978) and the individual's locus of control (the extent to which a person feels responsible for the outcome and consequences of his or her own behaviour) can also have an effect on behaviour and response to counselling. An 'internal' person sees him- or herself as being in control of what happens to him or her; an 'external' person sees 'powerful others', or uncontrollable forces, as determining and shaping his or her behaviour. The identification of a client's 'locus of control' is an important first step in the counselling procedure, and is a common theme in the informal and formal counselling procedures with young people in residential care, who specifically experience problems around the issue of the control of behaviour (Easson 1969; Moordock 1979). For example, 'external' clients expect therapists to give advice, and 'internal' clients make more effective use of advice and information given to them. Client expectations also extend to the content and structure of the counselling process: they expect a greater understanding of themselves, a provision of suggestions they have not already noted or thought of as opposed to the therapist telling his or her own personal reactions to client problems, sitting quietly and saying little or providing a new set of values (Tuss and Greenspan 1979).

TRAINING FOR COUNSELLING

There are many formulations of training programmes for developing and enhancing counselling and helping skills. The use of role play, group discussion, and the rehearsal of specific helping skills such as 'continuing' or 'leading' skills (maintenance of communication and attempts to change or shape the relationship with specific statements or questions), and the capacity to understand and hear, and feel and sense what another person is saying can be used to integrate a set of effective enabling skills. Danish and Hauer (1977) stress the importance of listening skills. If properly developed, these skills enable a counsellor to understand the meaning of what the young client is trying to say. Once the counsellor has developed that understanding, he or she will be able to share and communicate that understanding in a way that is both supportive and constructive. With regard to the place of counselling in the residential establishment, it has to be emphasized that counselling is not just a formal activity that takes place at a specific time. In fact, for youngsters who experience severe anxiety about personal problems and the implications of self-disclosure, 'formal' counselling is possibly the least productive approach. Most residential treatment models (Redl and Weinman 1952; Diggles 1970; and Barish and Schonfeld 1973) emphasize the use of the total milieu as the focus for helping. Alternatively most effective helping is likely to occur when the young person feels most safe and least threatened. Also, many young people defend against the anxiety averted by the helping process by forming defences that also serve the function of keeping staff at a distance (Rinsley 1971). Young people in care will often tell a wide range of staff about some but not all of the issues that confront them and staff must meet regularly and be able to communicate fully, freely, and non-defensively in order to piece together a picture of the child's world, behaviour, attitudes, and expectations (Menninger Foundation Staff 1971). Rinsley (1971) called this defence 'transference diffusion', which is complicated by the fact that some young people are capable of manipulating staff into intra-team conflicts so that valuable information is not shared properly. At the same time, the young client may have experienced some relief from having disclosed issues to the 'team', as it were, and will want to see how the staff group handles and makes sense of the information. Training programmes will need to incorporate this element of team communication skills into a proper residential counselling programme.

There is evidence to show that specific training patterns significantly help the acquisition of counselling skills. Kuna (1975) found that the simple activity of reading a hand-out on counselling strategies can help in the learning of simple verbal interviewing skills, and that the modelling of skills by the trainer, in conjunction with verbal instructions, can, over time, significantly enhance the maintenance of such skills.

Micro-counselling training models (Peters *et al.* 1978) use a programme of didactic instruction in counselling skills that depends on written and/or video models, role-play practice, observer feedback, and remedial practice. Peters *et al.* found that certain aspects of this package (i.e. written and verbal models) were effective in enabling counselling trainers to acquire counselling strategies, to retain skills on a short-term basis, and to generalize the use of those skills to unrehearsed and novel situations. Clairborn (1979) emphasizes the role of interpretation rather than restatement on perceived counsellor effectiveness. Counsellors who made interpretations about client behaviour rather than simply restating what had been said were seen as more trustworthy and expert (because it seems he or she has something to say). Using such responsive verbal cues made counsellors seem more attractive and significant to clients, as long as non-verbal cues were congruent with verbal messages. However, it is risky to use interpretations without having a formal body of knowledge about theoretical models of both adolescent development and counselling strategies, especially as a disturbed adolescent may find the content of such interpretation either not useful, or indeed, threatening. Also, there could be possibilities in this situation for staff to use the treatment process to enhance their own standing and self-esteem rather than making it specifically valuable to the young client by providing the help that he or she needs.

MODELS OF COUNSELLING

Many theoretical and practical approaches to counselling now exist, with evidence to both their usefulness and their areas of particular relevance for treating specific types of client problems (Greenwald 1973; Keat 1974; Lembo 1976). However, in the last few years increasing attention has been given to the importance of attending to the personal models of counselling that individuals develop over time and with experience. Brammer (1973) also points to a 'growing eclecticism' among counsellors that leads to a 'unique, flexible but working style in a consistent manner'.

In a more detailed examination of this process, Leventhal and Slemburg (1977) proposed a model of psychotherapeutic operations that attempted to explain the findings that different helping styles based on very different conceptual frameworks were capable of achieving similar levels of results. Very simply, the model states that therapists enter a career with a theoretical model as a basis for understanding their patients and for developing treatment techniques for client's problems, but that the specific nature of the therapist-client interaction enables the therapist to observe and store a vast amount of empirical, day-to-day information about how the client changes in response to the therapist's specific actions as a helper. The therapist builds up a 'statistical table', as it were, of relationships between his or her helping behaviours as they interact with a range of clients with different problems. A crucial feature of this model is that therapists are observing real data about cause and effect in the helping relationship. Theoretical formulations provide the new therapist with a set of 'security operations' upon which he or she can rely. However, with experience, the importance and influence of these models diminishes in the face of real experience with clients. Such models are, of course, invaluable in aiding intra-therapist communication, and residential teams, like any other treatment team, need to develop a common language and set of assumptions about their work. However, in-service training should make good use of the practical models of help that staff have developed in their experience, so that a model can be developed that is meaningful to all concerned.

Postscript

Within community homes there are about 400 secure places. However, the special skills required for working in such units are little taught on courses for residential social workers. By secure unit we mean one in which there is some degree of perimeter security that may be provided either by locked doors and windows or by an outside wall, or by both. In the main, young people who end up in such units will have demonstrated violent behaviour (that is, behaviour that damages or threatens to damage either themselves or other people), or they will be young people who have been so out of control (for example, through persistent absconding) that they are thought to be in moral danger. Working with such young people in closed conditions over long periods of time is profoundly exhausting and anxiety-provoking and it can result in members of the staff themselves behaving in irrational ways. The stresses that staff have to bear in these units are little appreciated by legislators and administrators. Indeed, there is a way in which the staff of secure units cannot do the right thing as far as society as a whole is concerned. The staff of secure units frequently find themselves under attack. One section of society might accuse them of being too restrictive and imprisoning young people whilst another section of society accuses them of being too slack in discipline and of mollycoddling young delinquents. Secure units can very readily become a political issue. Local and national politicians eager to assert law and order may press for secure units to become more prison-like, whilst others may regard delinquent behaviour amongst young people as being the result of society's ills which need to be corrected rather than for the young people to be, as they would see it, punished. In the midst of the arguments the needs of the individual young people, and of the staff trying to care for them, tend to get lost.

People who work with adolescents in secure units face all the problems that have been discussed in this book (see particularly Chapter 2). There are, however, some special problems that need to be highlighted.

(1) Isolation

In order to become skilful in the handling of profoundly disturbed adolescents, workers in secure units need to stay in such units for at least a couple of years. Since a sense of stability and permanence is particularly important for such units, a significant proportion of staff (particularly the more senior members) will need to be in a post for much longer than two years in order to train recruits and to be available to support less-experienced workers. There is, however, a danger in working within the confines of a secure unit over a long period of time. Because some of the young people in secure units will have to stay there for many months, both staff and young people can become divorced from the outside world. Behaviour that by the standards of the outside world may seem idiosyncratic and maladaptive to the difficulties of day-to-day life may start to be accepted as normal. A similar problem is encountered in old-fashioned mental hospitals where staff and patients may live in close proximity for many years and may begin collusively to set up a little world that becomes disengaged from the mainstream of life; both patients and staff find it difficult to move out into rehabilitation or into other jobs. The danger of such institutionalization, both for the inmates of secure units and the staff working with them, can be reduced considerably if a determined effort is made by the managers of the institution to ensure that staff regularly go on external training courses and that they are constantly asked to discuss their work with observers coming into the institution. Also, where possible and so long as it is safe for both the adolescent and the outside community, visits outside the institution should be arranged for the adolescent.

In general, all closed units should have a strong managing

body together with designated outside observers both to support the residential staff and to alert them to institutional practices that may be damaging. It is impossible, because of the intensive nature of the experience of working in a closed unit, to be a disinterested observer of one's own practices. A survivor of one of the most dreadful 'closed units' ever devised, Auschwitz, has described how it became impossible to conceive of a world outside. For the inmates of Auschwitz the thousand-year Reich was a reality.

(2) Counselling in secure units

The behaviour of young people who end up in secure units can be so disturbed and disturbing that it draws attention away from underlying emotional difficulties fuelling the disturbance. One of the main unconscious functions of violent acting-out behaviour by an adolescent is to force the grown-ups who are caring for him or her to take responsibility for powerful and potentially overwhelming thoughts and feelings that the adolescent does not, as it were, want to own. It is as though the adolescent, in forcing staff to impose control, is absolving him- or herself from responsibility for his or her own violent thoughts and feelings. Premature attempts at counselling adolescents in which attempts are made to help the adolescent to look at him- or herself and his or her own behaviour, are, therefore, as a rule, vigorously resisted and may result in what is tantamount to a psychotic breakdown in which the adolescent's grasp of reality becomes impaired. A thirteen-year-old boy (an arsonist) had to be transferred as an emergency case to a secure unit from a very caring open unit where attempts had been made to get through to him via intensive counselling and regressive techniques (treating him as though he were a very much younger child). The boy found this regime overwhelming. He twice tried to set fire to his room and when the efforts of the counsellors were redoubled in order to help him through this phase, he ended up by quite literally trying to crawl up the walls of his room and saying that the staff were trying to kill him. He settled rapidly after a transfer to a secure unit of another institution in which he felt safe because, initially at least, he was not pressured into trying to forge intense relationships with staff.

Donald Rinsley (1971) has described the way in which very disturbed and violent adolescents may be threatened by a feeling of what Fliess (1972) has called 'hypersymbiosis' (the adolescent feels merged with, or overwhelmed by, the personality of another person's getting too close to them). For some violent adolescents, therefore, the acting-out behaviour is an attempt to keep other people at a distance. A sixteen-year-old girl had been admitted to eleven different residential establishments in two and-a-half years before finally being transferred to a secure unit. This example of bad social work practice was the result of a succession of social workers failing to appreciate that the girl, after a honeymoon period of a couple of days, felt compelled to violently reject adults who tried to get close to her. The rejection was not simply an attempt to test whether adults would care for her whatever she did, it was an attempt to prevent herself from being swamped by thoughts and feelings in relation to other people that were so powerful they threatened a psychotic breakdown of the sort described above.

Whilst counselling and indeed more intensive psychotherapy should be available to young people in secure units, the timing of its implementation and its significance for an individual adolescent must be carefully thought out, if necessary with a trained psychotherapist.

(3) Assessment of dangerousness

The forensic psychiatrist Peter Scott (1977) described dangerousness as a dangerous concept. The staff of secure units are, nevertheless, frequently called upon to make assessments of the dangerousness of the young people in their care. When, for example, may a particular young person be allowed out on visits and when may he or she be discharged? The assessment of dangerousness is particularly critical of course in the case of young people who have murdered. The fact is that with our present level of understanding, assessment of dangerousness is crude and to some extent hit and miss.

All seriously violent adolescents should be seen by a psychiatrist because very rarely violent behaviour may indicate a serious underlying psychiatric disorder such as schizophrenia. A nineteen-year-old admitted to a general medical ward because of slight chest and abdominal pains suddenly started to attack the nurses and other patients. He ended up by smashing a urine bottle over his own head and trying to jump out of the window. On examination by a psychiatrist, he was found to be in the throes of schizophrenic thought disorder and was suffering from auditory hallucinations in which Iris, the Goddess of the Rainbow, was calling to him. A number of studies (for example that of Kozol *et al*. 1972) have shown that assessors of dangerousness tend to err on the safe side. Kozol *et al.*'s study (of adult men) found that only one in three offenders deemed as dangerous perpetrated violent acts following their discharge. Whilst this may be (statistically) comforting, there is a difficulty in that our present methods of assessment are unable to tell us which one of the three will, in practice, become violent.

One of the best indicators of future behaviour is past behaviour. An adolescent who has been violent in the past has therefore a greater chance than a non-violent adolescent of being violent in the future. It is important, therefore, in assessing dangerousness to collate carefully all past records of the adolescent's behaviour and to canvass the opinions of all professionals who have had contact with the adolescent and his or her family. Careful detective work of this sort can give a much more accurate picture of an adolescent than a series of assessment interviews. A fourteen-year-old boy was referred to a psychiatrist for assessment because he had threatened another boy in his school with a knife. The teachers felt there was something especially troubling about this boy but they were uncertain of their feelings because in this particular school, situated in a very tough neighbourhood, it was not uncommon for boys to carry offensive weapons. At interview, the boy (whose parents came from an Asian country) presented as quietly spoken and indeed positively courteous. He lived with his mother (who was separated from his father) and younger brother and sister. His mother spoke little English and initially it was difficult to get her impressions of her son. However, when an interpreter (whom she came to trust) was brought into the case, the boy's mother told of a series of frightening episodes in which her son had threatened her and the younger children at knife point. A gentle manner and a kind-looking face are not to be used as any sort of indicator in assessing dangerousness. Potentially dangerous adolescents may often demonstrate a split quality in their personality. They may be capable of being kind and considerate and yet, at the same time, be potentially a hazard. Adolescents who have a 'secretive' quality about them, and to whom no member of staff feels especially close, may particularly have to be watched, as may those who demonstrate a single-minded interest in violent films and books.

Because our methods of assessing dangerousness are so hit and miss, it has been suggested (Pfohl 1978) that in the case of the more violent groups of offenders (murderers and arsonists for example), expert witnesses should present evidence for or against dangerousness to a lay panel who will decide, having deliberated on the evidence, whether or not an offender should be allowed back into society. In this way responsibility for assessment of dangerousness would be shared by experts with society as a whole.

CONCLUSION

The staff of adolescent secure units are asked to undertake one of the most difficult tasks in our society. The people who are responsible for them have a duty to train and to support such staff as fully as possible. If such support and training are available, work in a secure unit, although arduous, can be intensely fulfilling and the staff members of such an institution can establish a valuable *esprit de corps* which can be maintained by intensive training and continuous support.

References

Acton, W.P. (1970) Analytic Group Therapy with Adolescents. *Proceedings of the Fifth Conference of the Association for the Psychiatric Study of Adolescents*: 49–59.

Adler, J. (1971) Interpersonal Relationships in Residential Treatment Centres for Disturbed Children. *Child Welfare* **50**(4): 208–17.

Aichorn, A. (1944) *Wayward Youth*. New York: Viking Press.

Alderton, H. (1965) Communication, Learning and Therapeutic Processes in a Children's Psychiatric Hospital. *Journal of Canadian Psychiatric Association* **10**(5): 338–47.

Altmaier, E.M., Leary, M.R., Forsyth, D.R., and Ansel, J.C. (1979) Attribution Therapy: Effects of Locus of Control and Timing of Treatment. *Journal of Counselling Psychology* **26**(6): 481–86.

Ansbacher, H.L. (1968) The Concept of Social Interest. *Journal of Individual Psychology* **24**: 131–49.

Axline, V. (1947) *Play Therapy*. Cambridge, Mass.: Houghton Mifflin.

Balbernie, R. (1972) *Residential Work with Children*. London: Pergamon.

Bancroft, J. (1979) The Nature of the Patient-Therapist Relationship. *British Journal of Criminology* **19**(4): 416–19.

Bandler, J. and Grinder, J. (1976) *The Structure of Magic*. Vols 1 & 2. Palo Alto, Calif.: Science & Behavior Books.

Bandura, A. and Walters, R.H. (1963) *Social Learning and Personality Development*. New York: Holt, Rinehart and Winston.

Banet, A. (1976) Role Functions in a Group. In *Annual Handbook for Group Facilitators*. La Jolla, Calif.: University Associates.

Barish, J. and Schonfeld, W.A. (1973) Comprehensive Residential Treatment of Adolescents. In S.C. Feinstein and P.L. Giovacchini (eds) *Adolescent Psychiatry: Developmental and Clinical Studies*. Chicago, Ill.: University of Chicago Press.

Barrett, M.C. and McKelvay, J. (1980) Stresses and Strains on the Child Care Worker: A Typology for Assessment. *Child Welfare* **59**(5): 227–87.

Benson, S., Crooks, J., and Wolfenden, A. (1976) Staff Survival in Adolescent Units. *Proceedings of the International Conference on Adolescents*: 26–31. Edinburgh: Association for the Psychiatric Study of Adolescents.

Bergland, B.W. and Quatrano, L. (1973) Systems Evaluation in Counsellor Education. *Counsellor Education and Supervision* 128: 190–98.

Bettelheim, B. and Wright, B. (1972) Staff Development in a Treatment Institution. In G.H. Weber and B. Haberlein (eds) *Residential Treatment of Emotionally Disturbed Children*. New York: Behavioral Publications.

Bion, W.R. (1959) *Experiences in Groups*. London: Tavistock.

Blattner, H.A. (1975) *Acting In – Practical Applications of Psychodramatic Methods*. New York: Springer.

Boyd, L.A. and Roach, A.J. (1977) Interpersonal Skills of Communication Differentiating More from Less Satisfying Marital Relationships. *Journal of Counselling Psychology* 24(6): 540–42.

Bradford, L. P. (1976) *Making Meetings Work*. La Jolla, Calif.: University Associates.

Brammer, L. M.(1973) *The Helping Relationship: Process and Skills*. New York: Prentice-Hall.

Brandon, D. and Phillips, H. (1977) *Gamesters Handbook*. London: Hutchinson.

Briers, S. (1981) Breaking the 'Them-Us' Barrier. *Social Work Today* 12(22): 51–2.

Bruce, T.J.R. (1975) Adolescent Groups and the Adolescent Process. *British Journal of Medical Psychology* 48: 333–38.

Bruggen, P. (1979) Touch and Body Language in Family Therapy. *Journal of Family Therapy* 1: 221–29.

Bruggen, P. and Pitt-Aikens, T. (1975) Authority as a Key Factor in Adolescent Disturbance. *British Journal of Medical Psychology* 48(2): 153–59.

Carter, L., Haythorn, W., Shriver, B., and Lanzetta, J. (1968) The Behavior of Leaders and Other Group Members. In D. Cartwright and A. Zander (eds) *Group Dynamics: Research and Theory*. London: Tavistock.

Claiborn, C.D. (1979) Counsellor Verbal Intervention, Non-verbal Behaviour and Social Power. *Journal of Counselling Psychology* 26(5): 378–83.

Clark, D.H. (1974) *Social Therapy in Psychiatry*. Harmondsworth: Penguin.

Coleman, J.C. (1980) *The Nature of Adolescence*. London: Methuen.

Daley, M.R. (1979) Preventing Worker Burn-Out in Child Welfare. *Child Welfare* **58**(7): 443–50.

Danish, S.J. and Hauer, A.L. (1977) *Helping Skills*. New York: Human Sciences Press.

Davies, L. (1977) Feelings and Emotions in Residential Settings. *British Journal of Social Work* **7**: 26–39.

Diggles, M. (1970) The Child Care Counsellor: New Therapist in Children's Institutions. *Child Welfare* **49**(9): 509–13.

Dooley, D., Whalen, C.K., and Flowers, J.V. (1978) Verbal Response. Styles of Children and Adolescents in a Counselling Analog Setting – Effects of Age, Sex and Labelling. *Journal of Counselling Psychology* **25**(2): 85–95.

Douglas, T. (1976) *Groupwork Practice*. London: Tavistock.

—— (1978) *Basic Groupwork*. London: Tavistock.

—— (1983) *Groups*. London: Tavistock.

Douvan, E. and Adelson, J. (1966) *The Adolescent Experience*. New York: John Wiley.

Dunne, C., Bruggen, P., and O'Brian, C. (1982) Touch and Action in Group Therapy of Younger Adolescents. *Journal of Adolescence* **5**(1): 31–8.

Dymond J. and Donnelly, C. (1969) Executive Junctions of the Ego. *Archives of General Psychiatry, XX* March: 258.

Easson, W. (1969) *The Severely Disturbed Adolescent*. New York: International Universities Press.

Egan, G. (1975) *The Skilled Helper: A Model for Systematic Helping and Interpersonal Relating*. Monterey, Calif.: Brooks/Cote.

Eliot, T.S. (1963) *Collected Poems*. London: Faber & Faber.

Elkind, D. (1967) Egocentrism in Adolescence. *Child Development* **38**: 1025–034.

Erikson, E.H. (1968) *Identity: Youth and Crisis*. London: Faber & Faber.

Fant, R. and Ross, A. (1979) Supervision of Child Care Staff. *Child Welfare* **58**(10): 627–42.

Fiedler, F.E. and Korton, D.C. (1968) Personality and Situational Determinants of Leadership Effectiveness. In D. Cartwright and A. Zander (eds) *Group Dynamics: Research and Theory*. London: Tavistock.

Fliess, R. (1972) *Ego and Body Ego: Contributions to their Psychoanalytic Psychology.* New York: International Universities Press.

Frank, S.J. (1978) Just Imagine How I Feel: How to Improve Empathy through Training in Imagination. In J.L. Singer and K.S. Pope (eds) *The Power of Human Imagination.* Quoted in D. Watts Clinical Judgements and Clinical Training. *British Journal of Medical Psychology* **53**: 95–108.

Freud, A. (1958) Adolescence. *Psychoanalytic Study of the Child* **13**: 255–78.

Freud, S. (1978) Project for a Scientific Psychology. Vol I. Standard Edition. London: Hogarth Press.

Gilmore, M., Bruce, N., and Hunt, M. (1974) *The Work of the Nursing Team in General Practice.* London: Council for the Education and Training of Health Visitors.

Glass, C.R., Gothman, J.M., and Shmurak, S.H. (1976) Response Acquisition and Cognitive Self-Statement Modification Approaches to Dating Skills Training. *Journal of Counselling Psychology* **23**: 520–26.

Glasser, W.M. (1965) *Reality Therapy.* New York: Harper & Row.

Goffman, E. (1968) *Asylums.* Harmondsworth: Penguin.

Graham, P. and Rutter, M. (1973) Psychiatric Disorder in the Young Adolescent: A Follow-Up Study. *Proceedings of the Royal Society of Medicine* **66**: 1226–229.

Graves, J.R. and Robinson, J.H. (1966) Proximic Behaviour as a Function of Inconsistent Verbal and Non-Verbal Messages. *Journal of Counselling Psychology* **23**(4): 333–38.

Greenspoon, J. (1962) Verbal Conditioning and Clinical Psychology. In A.J. Bachrach (ed.) *Experimental Foundation of Clinical Psychology.* New York: Basic Books.

Greenwald, H. (1973) *Decision Therapy.* New York: Wyden.

Grisberg J., Stutman, S.S., and Hummel, J. (1979) Group Filial Therapy. *Social Work* **23**(2): 154–58.

Hanson, P. (1976) Giving Feedback: An Interpersonal Skill. In L.P. Bradford (ed.) *Making Meetings Work.* La Jolla, Calif.: University Associates.

Harris, D. and Anderson, S. (1979) The Need to Evaluate Residential Training. *Social Work Today* **10**(24): 27–9.

Hayman, A.W. (1965) Verbalization and Identity. *International Journal of Psycho-Analysis* **46**: 455–66.

Highlen, B. and Voight, N.L. (1978) Effects of Social Modelling, Cognitive Restructuring and Self-Management Strategies on Affective Self-Disclosure. *Journal of Counselling Psychology* 25(1): 21–7.

Hill, C.E. and Gormally, J. (1977) The Effects of Reflection, Restatement, Probe and Non-Verbal Behaviours on Client. *Journal of Counselling Psychology* 24(2): 92–8.

Hobbs, M. (1973) Long Term Care. Parts 1,2, and 3. *Residential Social Work* 13(4): 196–201; 13(5): 241–46; 13(6): 296–300.

Hoghugi, M. (1978) *Troubled and Troublesome: Coping with Severely Disordered Children*. London: Burnett Books.

Holtby, M.E. (1972) Expectations of Experienced Child Care Staff. *Child in Care* 12(9): 12–15.

Hunt, M. (1979) Possibilities and Problems of Interdisciplinary Teamwork. In M. Marshall, M. Preston-Shoot, and E. Winicott (eds) *Team-Work – For and Against*. Birminghan: BASW Publications.

Hyatt-Williams, A. (1971) The Occupation Risk of the Workers in the Field of Adolescent Psychiatry. *Proceedings of the Sixth Conference of the Association for the Psychiatric Study of Adolescents, Guildford, 1971*: 71–7.

Jacques, E. (1955) Social Systems as a Defense against Persecutory and Depressive Anxiety. In M. Klein, P. Heimann, and R. Money-Kyrle (eds) *New Directions in Psycho-Analysis*. London: Tavistock.

Jones, J.E. (1973) The Sensing Interview. *Annual Handbook for Group Facilitators*. La Jolla, Calif.: University Associates.

Jones, M. (1968) *Social Psychiatry in Practice: The Idea of the Therapeutic Community*. Harmondsworth: Penguin.

Karlins, M. and Andrews, L.M. (1975) *Biofeedback. Turning on the Power of Your Mind*. Tunbridge Wells: Abacus Press.

Keat, D.B. (1974) *Fundamentals of Child Counselling*. Boston: Houghton Mifflin.

Kelly, G.A. (1955) *A Theory of Personality*. New York: Norton.

Klein, M. (1973) Our Adult World and its Roots. In M. Hobbs *Residential Social Work* 13(6): 296–300.

Knopka, G. (1955) The Role of the Group in Residential Treatment. *American Journal of Orthopsychiatry* 35(4): 679–84.

Korton, D.C. (1968) Situational Determinants of Leadership Structure. In D. Cartwright and A. Zander (eds) *Group Dynamics: Research and Theory*. London: Tavistock.

Kozol, H.L., Boucher, A.M., and Garofalo, R.F. (1972) The Diagnosis and Treatment of Dangerousness. *Crime and Delinquency* **18**: 371–92.

Krasner, L. (1961) 'The Therapist as a Social Reinforcement Machine'. Paper read at 2nd Conference on Research into Psychotherapy. University of California, Chapel Hill.

Krause, K. (1974) Authoritarianism, Dogmatism and Coercion in Child Care Institutions: a Study of Staff Attitudes. *Child Welfare* **53**(1): 23–30.

Kuna, D.J. (1975) Lecturing, Reading and Modelling in Counsellor Restatement Training. *Journal of Counselling Psychology* **22**: 542–46.

Kurtz, R.R. and Jones, J.E. (1973) Confrontations: Types, Conditions and Outcomes. In *Annual Handbook for Group Facilitators*. La Jolla, Calif.: University Associates.

Latané, B., Williams, K., and Harkins, S. (1979) Social Loafing. *Psychology Today* October: 104–10.

Laufer, M. (1975) *Adolescent Disturbance and Breakdown*. Harmondsworth: Penguin.

Lembo, J.M. (1976) *The Counselling Process*. New York: Libra.

Leventhal, D.B., and Slemburg, K.M. (1977) Psychotherapy; Theory, Experience and Personalised Actuarial Tables. *British Journal of Medical Psychology* **50**: 361–65.

Lewis, H.R. and Streatfield, S. (1970) *Growth Games*. New York: Bantam Books.

Lichtenburg, J.W. and Hummel, T.J. (1976) Counselling and Stochastic Process: Fitting a Markov Chain Model to Initial Counselling Interviews. *Journal of Counselling Psychology* **23**(4): 310–15.

Lin, T-T. (1973) Counselling Relationships as a Function of Counsellors' Self-Confidence. *Journal of Counselling Psychology* **20**: 293–97.

McClelland, D.C. and Burnham, D.H. (1976) Power is the Great Motivator. *Harvard Business Review* **54** 100–10.

Maier, H.W. (1971) The Child Care Worker. In R. Morris (ed.) *Encyclopaedia of Social Work*. New York: National Association of Social Workers.

Maslach, C. (1976) Burned-Out. *Human Behaviour* September: 16–22.

Maslow, A.H. (1970) *Motivation and Personality*. New York: Harper & Row.

—— (1976) *The Farther Reaches of Human Nature*. Harmondsworth: Penguin.

Menninger Foundation Staff (1971) *Disturbed Children*. San Francisco, Calif.: Josey Bass.

Menzies, I.E.P. (1970) *The Functioning of Social Systems as a Defence against Anxiety*. London: Tavistock Institute of Human Relations.

Miechenbaum, D. and Goodman, J. (1971) Training Impulsive Children to Talk to Themselves. *Journal of Abnormal Psychology* **77**: 115–26.

Miller, E.J. and Gwynne, G.V. (1972) *A Life Apart*. London: Tavistock.

Millham, S., Bullock, R., and Hosie, K. (1980) *Locking up Children*. Farnborough: Saxon House.

Moordock, R. (1979) Evaluation in Residential Treatment: The Conceptual Dilemma. *Child Welfare* **58**(5): 293–303.

Moreno, J.C. (1936) *Principles and Practice of Recreational Therapy for the Mentally Ill*. New York: Barnes & Noble.

Moustakas, C. (1959) *Psychotherapy with Children: The Living Relationship*. New York: Harper & Row.

Norwicki, S. and Duke, M.P. (1978) Examination of Counselling Variables Within a Social Learning Framework. *Journal of Counselling Psychology* **25**(1): 1–8.

Parsons, R.W. (1966) Psychological and Behavioural Change in Delinquents following Psychotherapy. *Journal of Clinical Psychology* **22**: 337–40.

Peters, G.A., Cormier, L.S., and Cormier, W.H. (1978) Effects of Modelling, Rehearsal, Feedback and Remediation on Acquisition of a Counselling Strategy. *Journal of Counselling Psychology* **25**(3): 231–37.

Pfeiffer, J.W. (1973) Conditions which Hinder Effective Communication. In *Annual Handbook for Group Facilitators*. La Jolla, Calif.: University Associates.

Pfeiffer, J.W. and Jones, J.E. (1972–80) *Annual Handbook for Group Facilitators*. La Jolla, Calif.: University Associates.

—— (1975) Co-Facilitating. In *Annual Handbook of Group Facilitators*. La Jolla, Calif.: University Associates.

Pfohl, S.J. (1978) *Predicting Dangerousness*. Lexington, Mass.: D.C. Heath.

Pines, A. and Kafrey, D. (1978) Occupational Tedium in the Social Services. *Social Work* **23**(6): 499–507.

Polsky, H. (1963) *Cottage Six*. New York: Russell Sage.

Polsky, H. and Claster, D.S. (1968) *The Dynamics of Residential Treatment; Social Systems Analysis*. Chapel Hill, NC: The University of North Carolina Press.

Redl, F. and Wineman, D. (1952) *Controls from Within*. Chicago: Aldine.

Reilly, A.J. (1974) Individual Needs and Organizational Goals. In J.W. Pfeiffer and J.E. Jones (eds) *Annual Handbook for Group Facilitators*. La Jolla, Calif.: University Associates.

Reilly, A.J. and Jones, J.E. (1974) Team-Building. In J.W. Pfeiffer and J.E. Jones (eds) *Annual Handbook for Group Facilitators*. La Jolla, Calif.: University Associates.

Remarque, E.M. von (1963) *All Quiet on the Western Front*. St. Albans: Mayflower Books.

Reutsch, J. (1972) *Disturbed Communication*. New York: Norton.

Rinsley, D.B. (1971) Theory and Practice of Intensive Residential Treatment of Adolescents. In S.C. Feinstein *et al*. (eds) *Adolescent Psychiatry*. Vol.I. New York: Basic Books.

—— (1980) *Treatment of the Severely Disturbed Adolescent*. New York: Jason Aronson.

Rogers, C. (1951) *Client-Centred Therapy*. Boston: Houghton Mifflin.

Roth, P. (1971) *Portnoy's Complaint*. London: Corgi Books.

Rotter, J. B. (1954) *Social Learning and Clinical Psychology*. Englewood Cliffs, NJ: Prentice-Hall.

—— (1975) Some Problems and Misconceptions Related to the Construct Internal v. External Control of Reinforcement. *Journal of Consulting and Clinical Psychology* **43**: 56–67.

Rubenstein, D. and Weiner, O.R. (1975) Co-therapy and Teamwork Relationships in Family Psychotherapy. In G.H. Zuk and I. Boszormenyi-Naji (eds) *Family Therapy and Disturbed Families*. Palo Alto, Calif.: Science & Behavior Books.

Rubin, R. (1972) Games and Simulations: Materials, Sources, and Learning Concepts. In J.W. Pfeiffer and J.E. Jones (eds) *Annual Handbook for Group Facilitators*. La Jolla, Calif.: University Associates.

Rutter, M. (1979) *Changing Youth in a Changing Society*. London: The Nuffield Provincial Hospitals Trust.

Salinger, J.D. (1951) *Catcher in the Rye*. London: Hamish Hamilton.

Schapiro, D.A. (1957) Some Implications of Psychotherapy Research for Clinical Psychology. *British Journal of Medical Psychology* **68**: 199–206.

Schapiro, S. and Tyrka, H. (1975) *Trusting Yourself*. Englewood Cliffs, NJ: Prentice-Hall.

Schutz, W.C. (1967) *Joy*. New York: Grove Press.

Schwartz, R.M. and Gottman, J.M. (1976) Toward a Task Analysis of Assertive Behaviour. *Journal of Counselling Psychology* **44**: 910–20.

Scott, P.D. (1977) Assessing Dangerousness in Criminals. *British Journal of Psychiatry* **131**: 127–42.

Selye, H. (1956) *The Stress of Life*. New York: McGraw-Hill.

Shaffer, D. (1974) Suicide in Childhood and Early Adolescence. *Journal of Child Psychology and Psychiatry* **15**: 275–92.

Shaw, S.H. (1973) The Dangerousness of Dangerousness. *Medicine Science and Law* **13**: 269–71.

Sherwood, J.J. (1972) An Introduction to Organizational Development. In J.W. Pfeiffer and J.E. Jones (eds) *Annual Handbook for Group Facilitators*. Iowa: University Associates.

Sinclair, I. (1971) Hostels for Probationers. *Home Office Research Unit Project*. London: HMSO.

Skynner, A.C.R. (1976) *One Flesh: Separate Persons*. London: Constable.

Spooner, S.E. and Stone, S.C. (1977) The Maintenance of Specific Counselling Skills over Time. *Journal of Counselling Psychology* **24**: 66–71.

Stanton, A.H. and Schwartz, M.S. (1954) *The Mental Hospital*. London: Tavistock.

Steinberg, D., Merry, J., and Collins, S. (1978) The Introduction of Small Group Work to an Adolescent Unit. *Journal of Adolescence* **1**(4): 331–44.

Stepsis, J. (1974) Conflict Resolutions Strategies. In J.W. Pfeiffer and J.E. Jones (eds) *Annual Handbook for Group Facilitators*. La Jolla, Calif.: University Associates.

Stevenson, O. (1977) *Social Work Research Project*. Universities of Keele, Bristol, and Aberdeen. Published jointly by DHSS, DHSS (N. Ireland), and Social Work Service (Scotland).

Storr, A. (1979) *The Art of Psychotherapy*. London: Secker & Warburg.

Sulzer, E.S. (1962) Reinforcement and the Therapeutic Contract. *Journal of Counselling Psychology* **9**(3): 310–19.

Sweeney, M.A. and Cottle, S. (1976) Non-Verbal Acuity: A Comparison of Counsellors and Non-Counsellors. *Journal of Counselling Psychology* **23**(4): 394–97.

Taylor, J. (1979) Introducing Team Nursing. *Nursing Times* November 22: 34–6.

Treichman, A. and Whittaker, J. (eds) (1974) *The Other 23 Hours*. Chicago: Aldine.

Truax, C.B. and Carkhuff, R.R. (1967) *Towards Effective Counselling and Psychotherapy*. Chicago: Aldine.

Tuss, C.R. and Greenspan, B. (1979) The Transmission and Acquisition of Values in the Residential Treatment of Disturbed Adolescents. *Adolescence* 14(55): 41–8.

Walton, R. (1978) Training for Risk-Taking: Applications in Residential Care. *Social Work Service Journal* December: 1–5.

Watkins, T. (1979) Staff Conflicts over the Use of Authority in Residential Settings. *Child Welfare* 58(3): 205–16.

West, D.J. (1967) *The Young Offender*. Harmondsworth: Penguin.

Whittaker, J. and Treichman, A.E. (1972) *Children Away from Home*. Chicago: Aldine.

Winnicott, D.W. (1971) *Playing and Reality*. London: Tavistock.

Wolpé, J. (1969) *The Practice of Behaviour Therapy*. New York: Pergamon Press.

Wotherspoon, C.M.C. (1972) Making Authority a Positive in Residential Treatment. *Child Welfare* 51(10): 636–44.

Wood, J. (1976) Leadership as Persuasion and Adaptation. In J.W. Pfeiffer and J.E. Jones (eds) *Annual Handbook for Group Facilitators*. La Jolla, Calif: University Associates.

Wood, J. (1977) Constructive Conflict in Discussions: Learning to Manage Disagreements Effectively. In J.W. Pfeiffer and J.E. Jones (eds) *Annual Handbook for Group Facilitators*. La Jolla, Calif.: University Associates.

Yalom, I. (1958) *The Theory and Practice of Group Psychotherapy*. New York: Basic Books.

Zanski, J.J., Sweeney, T.J., and Bascikowski, R.S. (1977) Counsellor Effectiveness as a Function of Counsellor Social Interest. *Journal of Counselling Psychology* 24(1): 1–5.

Zarie, T.E. and Boyd, R.C. (1977) An Evaluation of Modelling and Experiential Procedures for Self-Disclosure Training. *Journal of Counselling Psychology* 24(1): 118–24.

Name Index

Subject Index